# MASQUERADERS MUSICIANS and the OLD TIME ST. CROIX CHRISTMAS FESTIVAL

KAREN C. THURLAND

AuthorHouse™
1663 Liberty Drive
Bloomington, IN 47403
www.authorhouse.com
Phone: 833-262-8899

Because of the dynamic nature of the Internet, any web addresses or links contained in this book may have changed
since publication and may no longer be valid. The views expressed in this work are solely those of the author and do
not necessarily reflect the views of the publisher, and the publisher hereby disclaims any responsibility for them.

Any people depicted in stock imagery provided by Getty Images are models,
and such images are being used for illustrative purposes only.
Certain stock imagery © Getty Images.

Cover Photo: Wild Indian masqueraders on King Street in Frederiksted, St. Croix.
Margo Graff Photo Collection          St. Croix Landmarks Society

Back Cover Photo: The AyAy Masqueraders of St. Croix.
Photo by Gerard Doward

This book is printed on acid-free paper.

ISBN: 978-1-6655-7814-1 (sc)
ISBN: 979-8-8230-0090-1 (hc)
ISBN: 978-1-6655-7815-8 (e)

Library of Congress Control Number: 2022923333

Print information available on the last page.

Published by AuthorHouse  04/24/2023

authorHOUSE®

# ACKNOWLEGEMENTS

I am extremely grateful to the people who contributed their time and assistance with the development of this book. Thanks to Anne Thurland, Gerard Doward, Josephine Hector and Carol Wakefield for their review of the manuscript and their valuable suggestions. Special thanks to Anne Thurland for the image and photo restorations. As always, I am forever thankful to the people who graciously provide their personal stories and family photographs. Special thanks to Joan Felix at the St. Croix Landmarks Society's Research Library. Without them this book would not be possible. A sincere thanks to Joan Paulus for her editing work.

The publication of this book has been made possible through funding from the Virgin Islands Academic & Cultural Awards Endowment.

# CONTENTS

# INTRODUCTION

Masqueraders, particularly the Wild Indians, scared me when I was young because they wore hideous-looking wire mesh face masks, carried tomahawks and hit the street pavement with whips. I will never forget the sound the whips made when they hit the street pavement. The sound of the drums coming down King Street alerted everyone that masqueraders were coming to entertain us and of course to scare a few children. The bright colorful costumes with the mirrors and the hats with the long feathers always caught my attention. Those are the masquerades I remember from my childhood days in Christiansted, St. Croix.

My parents, Will and Modesta Thurland, spoke fondly about Viggo Roberts masquerading as a Bull and also as a Devil. They told me about him dressing in bulrush using dried plantain leaves when he danced as a Bull. Over the years, they recalled an incident that occurred with Paddy Moore, a Frederiksted masquerader, who someone set his bulrush costume on fire and he ran and jumped in the sea. Lucky for him he was not badly burned. Masquerading in Christiansted town was entertaining and exciting, except children were afraid of the masked performers. The masked dancers often ran after children or would go up to them swinging their whips.

As a young girl living in Christiansted town I looked forward to the colorful street performances on holidays when I did not have to go to school. The sights and sounds amazed me and town life has always been a happy time in my life's journey. This book is a tribute to all the street performers who carried on our African heritage despite attempts by colonial authorities to suppress gatherings and holiday observances during enslavement and afterwards.

Harold Willocks, a Superior Court judge and historian, in his book *The Umbilical Cord* wrote about masquerades:

> Every year on Christmas, Easter, Labor Day, Christmas Second Day, Easter Monday, and Whit Monday, people would dress in costumes, play music and dance in the streets. This was called masquerade. It usually lasted from 2:00 pm until 6:00 pm. The participants would have to get permission from the police station.
>
> Masquerade was comprised of different troops like Mother Hubbard, the Flagpole, David and Goliath, Down South, Pirates, Wild Indians, Mocko Jumbie, and Donkey Want Water.
>
> Masquerade had become so set in the Virgin Islands, that Title 23 Section 372 (6) of the Virgin Islands Code specifically addresses the issue of masquerading. It states as follows:
>
>> (b) Permission for masquerading on the streets, roads, or other public places will be granted only on the Day after Christmas, New Year's Day, Transfer Day, Easter Monday, Whit Monday, and Fourth of July, and such other days as the Commissioner of Public Safety may fix with the approval of the governor.
>
> This section was based upon the Ordinance of the Colonial Council for St. Croix, which was approved June 15, 1929.

While conducting research for this book I revisited a few publications of Richard Schrader Sr., examining stories pertaining to masquerading over the years on St. Croix. The books that were extremely useful were *Notes of a Crucian Son, Maufe Quelbe and t'ng,* and *Under De Taman Tree.* In those books, Schrader provides a view of life as it was on St. Croix from the 1920s to modern times. The publication *Ole Time Masquerading in the U.S. Virgin Islands* by Robert W. Nicolls gives valuable insights about masqueraders, their costumes, music and dance traditions. Another important work is *The Glory Days of Frederiksted* by Our Town Frederiksted which provides a wealth of information about the masquerading traditions in that town, as well as, biographical information on some Festival troupe leaders.

A recent publication I discovered *One Grand Noise: Boxing Day in the Anglicized Caribbean World* examines masquerading traditions on Christmas Second Day throughout the Anglicized Caribbean World. Boxing Day was an English bank holiday. The author Jerrilyn McGregory describes her work as an ethnographic interrogation of Boxing Day in the Bahamas, Belize, Bermuda, St. Croix, and St. Kitts. She explained that "the Caribbean region have carnival and festivals, but each island has unique characteristics because of the people who were involved in the merrymaking and their interpretation of cultural African and European traditions and just wanting to have fun and enjoyment." I was excited to find out that Bermuda also had Wild Indian masqueraders.

Remember that even though St. Croix was governed by the Danish government the majority of the planters were English and there were Scot-Irish overseers on the plantations so our ancestors adapted European customs to our African cultural traditions of masquerading.

I would be remiss if I did not mention the outstanding work on Virgin Islands English Creole compiled into a dictionary by Lito Valls. This dictionary entitled, *What a Pistarckle!* has been utilized in all my research projects and publications.

The photographs in my book tell a story by themselves. I usually research the Axel Ovesen Collection at the Whim Museum Library because there is a wide variety of subjects among his photographs which span many years into the 20th century. In 2010, while searching through several photograph collections for my Power Point presentation "Masquerading Virgin Islands Style: A Pictorial View," I was pleasantly surprised to find a box of slides taken by Margo Graff sometime around 1956-57. My discovery yielded slides of Wild Indian masqueraders who look similar to those I so vividly remember seeing as a young girl in Christiansted. It was as if I had struck gold with those slides.

While perusing the St. Croix Festival booklet collection at the Estate Whim Library, I also found photographs that many people have never seen and would enjoy viewing. Photographs taken by Fritz Henle, the renowned German photographer, and Egil Klint, a native photographer, were featured in the early booklets and gave a colorful presentation of the Old Time Festival parades. These photographs are evidence of the pageantry, colors and festive activities that occurred during the Old Time Festivals on St. Croix.

My father Will Thurland had a collection of 8 millimeter films stored in canisters and as a child I remember him spreading a white sheet across a wall and showing them to his children on weekends or during the summer nights. He took pictures with his movie camera of Carnival parades in St. Thomas and Festival parades in Christiansted as well as family events. Those 8 millimeter films were transferred to a VHS tape at a Sears Store's special offer over twenty years ago. The VHS tape was stored away years ago prior to the hurricane season but, unfortunately, was not stored in a cool place. I recently had that tape sent away to have the mold removed and the pictures transferred to a DVD. The pictures are slightly faded, but I was excited to capture photos of my Aunt "Jenny" Thurland in her Bull costume with her Matador Troupe and several other parade entries.

Unfortunately, since the hurricanes of 2017, the Caribbean Collection at the Florence Williams Public Library has been closed due to damage done to the building making it impossible for me to read the microfilm copies of the *St. Croix Avis* and the *West End News* that are stored there. Newspaper coverage of parades provide colorful descriptions of troupes and floupes and gave other pertinent information and would have been vital to my research which highlights the early years of the St. Croix Christmas Festival, then known as the Old Time Christmas Festival. My primary objective was to complete this book for the 70th Anniversary of the St. Croix Festival.

The Old Time Christmas Festival began in 1952 and the year 2022 marks the 70th anniversary. Former Delegate to Congress Ron de Lugo had a radio program in St. Thomas with a character called "Mango Jones" who talked about reviving the celebrations of bygone years. The people on both islands heard him and planned their respective parades and other forms of entertainment. St. Thomas had their first Carnival on Labor Day in September of 1952 and the St. Croix organizers decided to have their Festival around the traditional masquerading days of Christmas Second Day and chose New Year's Day to end the festivities.

This book is divided into basically three sections featuring recollections of masqueraders and three performers, two outstanding musicians and a brief history of the early years of the Old

Time Christmas Festival from 1952 to the early sixties. Additionally, stories about several troupe leaders are included in this book.

The name of the Christmas festivities has changed over the years from the original Old Time Festival, St. Croix Christmas Festival, St. Croix Christmas Fiesta, St. Croix Carnival and back to St. Croix Christmas Festival and the Crucian Christmas Festival. There are no more Christmas Second Day or Boxing Day parades but the spirit of "Playing Mas" continues every year. The Festival activities entertain people from St. Croix and abroad who desire the pageantry, colors and fun of parades, food fairs, getting together with family and friends, or just a reason for those living off island to come home.

The idea of documenting St. Croix's festive activities and highlighting several performers and providing eyewitness accounts of masquerading and parade events evolved over time and I collected whatever interesting information I found. My hope is that readers would enjoy reading this book and future generations of Virgin Islanders will understand the historic and cultural traditions of our annual celebrations. This book is my contribution to the cultural literacy of the Virgin Islands.

# The Masqueraders Coming

M rs. Iris Williams Browne from Watergut remembers Monroe Clendenen with his Pirates and One Hand Dan masquerading and running after children. She stated, "Viggo Roberts came from Comanche Hotel Yard. The musicians who played in the scratch bands were Joe Knight and Zeke Tub. Ciple was a one-man band with his kerosene pan and he sometimes tried to sing in Spanish."

It is quite true that Ciple could sing Spanish songs because he had lived in the Dominican Republic for a few years. His name was Alexander Michael and he lived in the Watergut neighborhood of Christiansted. The Dominican Republic also have masqueraders who have roots in Nevis and other Caribbean islands.

Mrs. Browne continued, "Magnus, the mocko jumbie, when he took off his stilts had to sit on the roof of the Pink Fancy Hotel because he was so tall. In the 1940s, Nelthropp owned that building and people rented and lived there."

She recalled the joy of hearing the scratch bands. "On Christmas Eve night when church service was over you would hear the scratch bands. If they came and played on the street in front of your house they would be treated with sweetbread, ham and a local drink of guavaberry."

*Alexander "Ciple" Michael playing music on a kerosene pan while One Hand Dan blows a tail pipe.*
*Photo by Fritz Henle*             *Courtesy of Fritz Henle Estate*

*John "Magnus" Farrell dancing on his stilts high above the crowd in St. Thomas.*
*National Geographic Magazine*                                         *Fair Use*

Modesta Larsen Thurland in the book *The Neighborhoods of Christiansted: 1910 – 1960* fondly recalls masquerade days of long ago. Mrs. Thurland said, "I remember Ciple had a scratch band and he used to "knock a kerosene pan," and some of the masqueraders would sing about Queen Mary while they performed on the street. They would only perform on masquerade days."

When asked about women masqueraders she replied, "There was a lady by the name of Maybelle, but I don't remember her last name. And she used to dance with a troupe that wore a wire mask over their faces so you couldn't tell who they were. But this lady knew my family well, and when they had masquerades she would come to our house with the troupe and dance for my family. The dance was referred to as quadrille and the music was called scratch band music."

Recently, after her passing, I found a copy of an autobiography my mother had written years ago. She wrote, "I have so many good memories of growing up on St. Croix. Easter Monday was a big holiday on St. Croix and also the day after Christmas. The masqueraders came out on those days. The Bull was a man dressed in brown leaves and had a bull horn. Children would scream, "The Bull is out," and run and hide. I was awfully afraid of the Bull, because he used to chase children so I stayed home and looked at him through the window at No. 16 Church Street."

Mrs. Modesta Thurland described the music played for the masquerades. "I remember that Jamesie and Mr. Waterman had scratch bands. I listened to Jamesie and his scratch band when he would be playing on the street. On a big holiday like Easter Monday, all the masqueraders, like the Indians, the Bull, and the Mocko Jumbies, came out."

Edna Coff Belardo of Christiansted worked at the Sheltered Workshop at the Herbert Grigg Home for the Aged for several years with seniors. "I would go in the ward and a lot of the people were masqueraders and One Hand Dan and Viggo Roberts were patients there.

I remember in Christiansted, the masqueraders used to go up Company Street and I would go to my aunt, Miss Maude Bolling's house, across from the Steeple Building, to look at them. Viggo Roberts masqueraded by himself, not in a troupe. He portrayed either the Devil or the

Donkey. The masqueraders came out in the afternoon after lunch. My mother and I would sit on our gallery on Hill Street and when we heard the music, we would hurry down to Aunt Maude on Company Street to see them. I was afraid of the masqueraders because of their masks. The mocko jumbies were as tall as the upstairs window and I was afraid of them. Daddy always gave me some change to give them."

Mrs. Coff Belardo concluded, "On some holidays the masqueraders would come over the hill to our house because Daddy would give them money, usually dollar bills. They would come and dance in front of our house. The old time scratch band music was played by a band."

Monroe Clendenen, Jr., reminisced about his father Monroe Sr., a Christiansted goldsmith, and the Pirates. "My father had a Pirate troupe that performed down the streets in the late 1940s and the 1950s. I used to be with him during the practice sessions and he had rules. He was not easy with the troupe members. He sewed the costumes himself and some of the other members made their own costumes. I used to pick up the money that people threw at the group. The only time I didn't handle money was at the Old Year's dances at the Congressional Hall on Church Street because he collected that himself. He had a scratch band, the Phillipus Brothers, that played for the troupe. A few of the members were Rally, Joseph and Bascombe and they were pirates, too."

Joan Paulus, from Gallows Bay in Christiansted, remembers her mother taking her to see the masqueraders and asking what the Wild Indian masquerader was telling the children. Her mother Agnes signaled to one of the masqueraders and he came over. Joan said, "The Wild Indian asked me if I listen to what my mother tells me and I said yes. He said, "That's good. Well, keep on doing that," and he walked off. Masqueraders reinforced good behavior in children. Reflecting on that incident, I am reminded of the African saying, "It takes a village to raise a child." Everyone in the community participates in the raising of children and we were taught to respect all adults as we would our parents. We learned to say "Good Morning" and "Good afternoon" to our elders and we dared not forget our manners because our parents would find out and reprimand us."

The Pirates of Penzance Festival Troupe Led by Monroe Clendenen, Sr.
Courtesy of St. Croix Landmarks Society

Norma Dennis Mason, who grew up in the Western Suburbs neighborhood of Christiansted, recalled seeing masquerades. "I remember Joseph "Tarzan" Daniel and Viggo Roberts came around dressed as the Bull. Miss Andreas played the guitar or ukulele and would sing. Ciple used to hit a biscuit pan and sing songs that he himself composed. The masqueraders used to come around town on holidays and I was afraid of them and used to hide. They covered their faces with mesh wire. Parents would tell their children, "If you misbehave, I will put you outside." No child wanted to be on the street when the masqueraders came out.

She recalled that there were other street performers besides the masqueraders who danced in the streets. "Albert Halliday from Frederiksted would come up to Christiansted and perform an oratory demonstration with a Sears Roebuck catalog. Sometimes Tarzan did that too. I remember Magnus, a mocko jumbie, who came up from Frederiksted. He had on long clothes that covered his legs on the stilts and his face was covered with safe wire."

Mrs. Mason stated that the Lantern Parades in Christiansted started at Bassin Triangle and were held either after Christmas or a day before Christmas. "Those parades started around six o' clock and went down to the Wharf where the Festival Tent was situated. Some people came in regular clothes, while others came in costumes. Some wore big, old clothes and painted their faces and others cut up old clothes and had strips. When I was a little older my sister and I had on costumes and were allowed to go down King Street or stand on King Street by where the bakery is now.

First the musicians would walk and I remember later Ciple and other musicians sitting in a truck. Also, Mr. Petersen and the Ten Sleepless Knights, the original group, played music for the parades. Later, Helen Joseph continued the tradition and the musicians played in a truck."

Norma remembered the Lantern Parades. "I was seven years old when they first started the Lantern Parades. My family lived in Western Suburbs so I watched it up there. There were people with children in big strollers and everyone young and old were having a good time.

I remember carrying a Japanese lantern with a candle. Some people had lanterns with handles. What they did was they would take the round lantern and put it on a stick. As children we made lanterns out of construction paper, well the adults made bigger ones and some people ordered

Chinese and Japanese lanterns. Then they had a bamboo stick with a candle and held the lantern up in the air."

When asked why did the Festival committee did not continue the tradition on holding Lantern Parades Norma replied that she did not know why. She stipulated that the parades stopped when they started going to Parade Ground and were no longer held at the Christiansted Wharf.

Colette Woodson Burgess shared her recollection of Lantern Parades. "People put cans like a big juice or vegetable can on a stick. They punched holes in the cans and put a piece of wire to make a handle. They used a stick to hold the handle because they had a lit candle inside the can. It was mostly women who participated and a scratch band played music for those parades."

George Thurland Sr., remembers Viggo Roberts and other masqueraders performing in front of his grandparents' house at No. 1 Hospital Street in Christiansted. He stated, "They danced for a while on the street and I threw money at them from the porch. The masqueraders had mirrors sewed on their clothes and some wore a long gown. They had safe masks on their faces. Viggo sometimes dressed as a bat and would go to his home and come back down the street dressed as a Devil. Viggo would run after the kids and one time I saw him chase some kids around a house, he stopped and then went around the opposite side of the house to scare them."

George said his father Will Thurland told him that One Hand Dan would come close to you and spin around and around. You had to move or he would knock you down. George fondly recalled that a masquerader named Francois, who probably was from St. Kitts, asking him if he wanted to become a masquerader and he would train him. George said that he asked his mother and she said, "No."

"At the age of six or seven, I joined a clown troupe along with my brother Freddy (Gotfred). Our costumes were multicolored and had tiny bells sewed on the legs. I kept my costume for several years and would put it on when my family listened to the St. Thomas Carnival on the radio and jump up and down as though I was in the parade. My siblings and I marched in our yard to a masquerade beat we made by hitting on old biscuit pans with sticks."

*Colette Woodson Burgess carrying a madras covered lantern in the 2019 Lantern Parade in Christiansted.*
*Photo by Karen C. Thurland*

Reminiscing George stated, "The Lantern Parades came down King Street and my family and I used to walk to Government House to meet the parade. I believe masquerade music was played for the performers.

I remember the steel band tramps in Christiansted when the Trojans came down the hill. They stopped and played by my family's house on Hospital Street. My granny, Ruth Thurland, would give them guavaberry, sweet bread and bush rum. The Watergonians Steel Band also passed by the house."

Dimitri Copemann, a Quelbe musician and radio talk show host, reminisced about the masquerades of bygone years. "People did it for the fun of it and they made their own costumes. My mother told me about Viggo Roberts and the characters he used to portray. Monroe Clendenen was with the Pirates and he was also the Parade Marshall for the Festival."

Mr. Copemann provided the names of a few female masqueraders. "Miss Clementina "Clemmie" Moore from Watergut, who was married to "Soda" the musician, had a troupe that performed on holidays. In the 1940s, a Marian Joseph used to dance masquerade. There were several troupes led by women who had Mother Hubbard, the Party Girls set, and sometimes Queen Mary and they did not all wear masks. Anna Phillipus danced masquerade, and she also played the squash and could strum a little bit of guitar.

Joe Knight used to masquerade and he also played the saxophone. William Mullicks, an old man, played the flute and provided music for the masqueraders. Ralph "Rally" Phillipus used to do oratory performances and I remember seeing him once in the Christiansted Festival Village reading from a folded-up piece of cardboard.

Delvin Walters used to dance masquerade and I knew him as an older man when he was not dancing anymore. Huntt from Watergut used to dance also. Alexander "Hoosterman" Hendricks used to play masquerade music and danced too. I knew him to be in parades when I was in kindergarten or first grade. Somebody told me about a Benjamin Newton who came to St. Croix in 1896 from St. Kitts. I found out about Smokey Joe who used to dance the jig, but I don't know his name. A man named Powell from Colquohoun also danced masquerade."

*Masqueraders on Company Street in Christiansted, St. Croix.*
*Balfour Fleming Collection          St. Croix Landmarks Society*

*Masqueraders with their King dancing by Government
House in Christiansted, St. Croix, early 1900s.
Photo by Axel Ovesen       St. Croix Landmarks Society*

In the *St. Croix Avis* article of December 29, 1993, entitled *"Masquerading: A Crucian Christmas Tradition,"* Dimitri Copemann lists several Christiansted musicians of bygone years such as Cornelius "One Hand Dan" Lucas, Fuzzy Knight, "One Man Band" Thompson, Willie Danielson and the Simmonds Brothers.

The author's mother lived in Estate Colquohoun with her parents on a homestead plot and she often spoke of her neighbors, the Powell family. I spoked with Mrs. Sarah Powell James who still lives on that estate and she was very excited about my inquiry because it was her father who was a performer in the David and Goliath plays.

Mrs. James said, "Yes, my father James Powell used to do masquerade. He played Goliath and my uncle James Barnes, who was my mother's brother, played David. It was in the 30's and 40's and I was a little child but heard about it."

I asked her where did her father learn about David and Goliath. She replied that the story is in the Bible and he got the idea from Nevis where he was born. According to the United States Census Records for 1930 and 1940, James Powell is listed as a sugar farmer in Colquohoun.

Masquerading also took place on holidays in the St. Croix countryside. Several masqueraders entertained in their own estate village and also went to other estate villages or travelled to the towns to perform. Inez Halls Lang and Bodil Mason Simmonds who lived at Lower Bethlehem, Richard Schrader, Sr. from Colquohoun, and Josephine Hector from Golden Grove shared their childhood memories of the various masked performers.

Inez Halls Lang of Lower Bethlehem recalled her memories of masqueraders coming out on holidays when she was a young girl:

> They went from village-to-village masquerading at Christmas time. I was so scared of them that I and my siblings hid under the bed and never went out of the house to look at them. They knew we were afraid of them. One Hand Dan used to dress as an Indian and would come to our house and hit his hatchet against the wall to scare us. Of course, we did not come out of the house until he moved on through the village. If you were outside, he would come up to you scaring you.

*A Christmas celebration at Estate Hogensberg, circa 1880s.*
*AJ Blackwood Collection          St. Croix Landmarks Society*

Our village was near the sugar factory and the masqueraders used to come at different times of the day. One Hand Dan wore a skimpy bottom and top. He had a bandana on his head and stuck painted turkey feathers in it because turkey feathers were wider than chicken feathers. Some masqueraders took paint and marked their face and skin. One or two mocko jumbies used to come to the village.

Mrs. Lang also stated, "The May Pole dancers dressed in multi-colored clothes like madras also came to the village. Sundial Store in Christiansted, owned by Antonio Gonzales, sold that type of material."

Bodil Mason Simmonds of Lower Bethlehem recollected, "Children used to run from the Bull who came with a bill (a cutlass used for cutting cane) in his hand. He used to come into the village "Braggadam, Braggadam." He had something on his head with horns. I don't know who he was because he never took off his mask. The Wild Indians came dressed in a skirt of patchwork cloth and had feathers on their heads. I can't say who those people were behind the masks. They might even have been people from Bethlehem but as children we couldn't say who the people were because their faces were hidden with the masks."

When asked about a particular masquerader Bodil replied, "All I remember about Smokey Joe is that he had a donkey costume. I can't recall his name."

Richard Schrader, Sr., author of historical and cultural books on St. Croix, grew up in the country and has shared vivid memories of the masquerading groups that performed in Colquohoun and Bethlehem when he was young. He has written stories about several of these characters in his books. He described several of the masqueraders he saw as a youngster:

In the 40s, around Christmas and Easter, certain groups came in trucks, and some came on foot. Willie Carroll was the leader of the David and Goliath troupe that would come to the estates. This play was based on the Biblical story and was well received by people all over the Island.

Mr. Carroll was a tall man over six feet who weighed more than 200 pounds and dressed like a warrior with sheep skin around his head and around his arms. He carried a sword on his side and a large pole in his right hand. I remember him well jumping up and down. Ira Giddings played the part of young David and would have a slingshot in his hands.

Schrader recited what Goliath would say during the performance:

I sent to King Saul for a man to fight. He sent me a stripling youth just fit to dance with women! Goliath would pause and ask, "Boy! Am I a dog?"

"No," said David, "but a creature worse than a dog!"

Goliath would become angry and then plunge after David who side-stepped the giant and hit him with the stone from his slingshot.

Schrader further explained the performers and musicians who came out masquerading:

Musicians came with the performers. On Christmas morning you heard the music played by a band coming through the cane fields to the village and people would give them something to eat and drink after the performances. I think Estate Bethlehem had musicians. John Byron was one of them and Mr. Arthur Weeks made the tambourine bawl with his thumb. Smokey Joe came out of Bethlehem, and he would have an animal head with horns and a rope. He also had a chain tied around his waist with part of it dragging on the ground.

The Bull I might have seen at Bethlehem, but not in Fredensborg, where we mostly had David and Goliath and Mother Hubbard troupes. There was a lady who lived in the village, Miss Langley, who would wear a safe wire mask when she played masquerade, and I was afraid of her. I was about five years old and at the Children's Home Miss Agatha Krause, who was the cook, and Mrs. Tranberg Andrews would tell us, "I gon call Miss Langley for you."

*David and Goliath performers in costume with their weapons. Goliath wore a tall hat to appear much taller than David.*
*Photo by Axel Ovesen    St. Croix Landmarks Society*

*David and Goliath troupe dressed as soldiers for their street performance.*
*Photo by Axel Ovesen*          *St. Croix Landmarks Society*

Josephine Hector grew up in the village at Estate Golden Grove and fondly remembers the masquerades of the 1940s and 1950s. She explained, "The people who lived in the village worked as laborers planting, weeding, and cutting cane for the Virgin Islands Company (VICO), who owned the houses. The village had two long row houses and individual houses which had a space for planting provisions like potatoes and yams. At the end of the row of houses was a big tree, I think a Thibet, and there was where the masqueraders performed and danced for us. We were glad to see the masqueraders and hear the scratch band music because the only music played in our village was done by one or two men who had banjos and would occasionally play and sing for us.

> People used to come to masquerade at Golden Grove from Christiansted and other places. I have seen Viggo who was from Christiansted. Miss Dolly Faulkner

from Christiansted had a troupe and when they came to my village they would spread out a sheet so whomever came to see them perform would throw out money which consisted of coins or a dollar. Sometimes the wind blew away the paper money and someone would retrieve it and put a stone on top of it.

The women wore masks made out of mesh wire with eyes drawn on it. Those masks were very pretty but some could have been scary. They wore different color dresses, two matching with the same color. A nice pretty dress of either green, blue, red or other colors. They wore fancy clothes, very pretty with frills and tucks. It was well done.

You could count on Miss Dolly and her troupe coming on Easter Monday or Whit Monday, the big holidays. The musicians who came with them played the steel and squash. The music they played was to soothe the troupe.

Paddy Moore from Frederiksted was a musician and I think he played the guitar. I don't know if he ever was in a troupe but he might have been.

David and Goliath came around to the different estates with Mr. Willie Carroll playing the part of Goliath. His group performed the story from the Book of Samuel that is in the Bible. Mr. Robert Henry and Mr. Powell from Colquoquon were also involved in the play. Those involved in that play came from the country. The performers dressed up like they were in the army and were ready for war. They had silver things like swords. Goliath would say in a loud voice, "I ask for a man to fight with me and they sent me this bwoy." The young boy had stones in a bag that he would use against Goliath.

The masqueraders used to hire a truck to take them around to the different estate villages. Mr. Theovald Slater was of them they used to hire.

*A women's masquerade troupe dancing on Easter Monday at Estate Butler's Bay, circa 1956-57.*
*Photo by Margo Graff*          *St. Croix Landmarks Society*

*A scratch band providing music for the masquerade troupe at Estate Butler's Bay, circa 1956-57.*
*Photo by Margo Graff*                 *St. Croix Landmarks Society*

Josephine Hector also stated, "I liked Tea Meetings and also when someone died they had a Wake (a watch or vigil held over the body of a deceased person before burial) at night. You would get a biscuit and sausage and people sang hymns. There were kerosene pans with tea, coffee or bush tea for you to choose from. The participants sang and recited parts from the Bible."

Going from the countryside to the town of Frederiksted there are many stories about masqueraders down in the western section of St. Croix. Evelyn Richardson, who was born in Frederiksted in 1899, in her book *Seven Streets by Seven Streets* wrote about 'the special days: Easter Monday, Whit Monday (the day after Pentecost Sunday), and Christmas Second Day.' She explained, "As a child those days were spent in amusements, such as people masked and dressed in beautiful costumes and dancing in the streets with their individual bands of music. There were no formal parades but people would form troupes and dance from street to street. These masquerades took place in the early years of the nineteenth century.

Ms. Richardson wrote about a woman named Petronella and the children she would gathered into her troupe on holidays:

> The children usually ranged in ages from seven to ten years. We were dressed in pretty Mother Hubbards, with gaily trimmed bonnets with ribbons tied under our chins. We wore sandals that most mothers made of white canvas on the top and thick pasteboard soles. The townsfolk would always be looking to see Petronella and the children. She took us into the homes of many of the rich and not-so-rich. There we would dance and sing for them. They, in turn, gave us candy, lemonade and buns.

She further described the musicians and masqueraders who visited homes to dance and were given money and drinks:

> Besides these masqueraders, there were mocko jumbies (high stilt walkers), the Wild Indians, and the Devil who was dressed in a black robe with bull horns lashed onto his head and an iron chain around his waist with a hand bell. His face was painted red and he gave a loud roar as he came near you. There was the David and Goliath troupe with colorful costumes and they used a few phrases from the Bible. They drew quite an audience around them.

*Masqueraders with a plait pole in costumes and wearing masks, 1924.*
*Photo by Axel Ovesen                    St. Croix Landmarks Society*

*A masquerader in a bulrush skirt and another in a coat and top hat dancing to the music of a scratch band.*
*Courtesy of Delta Dorsch*                                                   *St. Croix Landmarks Society*

Evelyn Richardson provided some historical knowledge about mocko jumbies. "The first mocko jumbies came from St. Kitts, Antigua and Barbados during the early 1900's. The greatest of them was Marshall, who came from Barbados. He was the lobster man in this town for many years."

Al Franklin, former president of Our Town Frederiksted, recalled his knowledge of masquerading in *The Glory Days of Frederiksted and* spoke about some of the performers:

> Masquerade was the delight of many, and the fear of a few. In the early afternoon, around two to three o' clock, they would start coming out from Harden Gut road, at Wheel of Fortune, they would be coming from "Over the Pan," Prosperity, New Town, from the Southside, and from Foster. Albert Halliday was a comedian who made up stories which he read from a Sears Roebuck catalogue, and he wore an

old cut-a-way coat, a high derby hat, and his cravat. Halliday made people laugh, moving from house to house, where people threw money out of their windows at him.

*Albert Halliday with a sales catalogue comic and social commentary in Frederiksted.*
*Photo by Axel Ovesen*                                        *St. Croix Landmarks Society*

Anyone reminiscing about the masquerades of long ago must talk about Paddy Moore. Mr. Franklin wrote, "Most popular and feared by children was Paddy Moore. Paddy could make the most fearsome masks, and dressed in bulrush, banana leaves, crocus bag; he was most creative, and he could dance."

Mr. Franklin described their dress but did not document the names of the women who had masquerade troupes:

> The women troupes were the highlight of the masquerades. Though they wore masks, you could tell from their dancing and the names of the troupes who they were. Their costumes were their trademark, and they competed for the best dressed. They wore headpieces, dresses, bells, mirrors, and they carried whips and other trinkets. The troupes usually came from the various villages throughout the island, and they did this all for the fun of it.

Clifford Christian described the masqueraders in a story in *The Glory Days of Frederiksted* publication:

> A masquerader was, for example, a mocko jumbie on stilts or someone dressed like a Wild Indian. Masqueraders would dress up in beads and bright colors with a group drumming and playing music. Lots of bands would come playing banjos. People like Mary Catherine would sing Cariso music. She had a butter pan and she sang all the old time songs. Cariso is cultural, expressing something about oneself, family, or a community member. People would always get together and have fun expressing themselves during holidays. People would come down from the country and share the fun times as well.

Alexander Petersen, who grew up in North Side where Paddy Moore also lived, was quoted in Richard Schrader's *Under De Taman Tree* talking about Paddy masquerading in Frederiksted town:

> Paddy was born on St. Croix but lived in Santo Domingo. He was an actor and cultural bearer, a very creative man, and Crucian to his heart. Masquerading was

his pleasure and Paddy made and wore attractive costumes. And he made them from just about anything he could get his hands on like banana leaves, bulrush (a plant which grows near water), canvas cloth, goat and sheep skin. He used glass, metal, and wood to create a particular effect. For example, the pieces of glass sewn to his attire reflected the sun rays as he danced about.

He was seldom without a mask and, as the artist he was, he used paint to its full advantage. And he was never without leggings which were made from women's old stockings. These ran from his knees and went over his bare feet to his instep.

Petersen described how Paddy made his drums. He taught Petersen and others to make the kettle drum, snare drum, and bass drum:

Whenever Paddy made something, he started from scratch. When making a drum he would kill a goat and place the skin in the sun to dry until it became very hard. He would then cover the hair with sand, take a gadget with a beveled edge (which he had made himself), and rub the sand over the skin, removing all of the hair. He would rub it until it was completely white. Next, he would wet the skin, making it supple to fit over the keg which he had already made.

Frank "Frankie Pete" Petersen gave his memories of Paddy Moore, whom he knew from his childhood days, in *Under De Taman Tree* by Richard Schrader:

Paddy Moore was the last person to wear African costumes during the holidays while masquerading. He was usually dressed in an outfit made from bulrush or banana leaves. While masquerading, Paddy would be dancing to the music from the flute, goatskin drum, steel, squash, and tailpipe. Sometimes Paddy played the goatskin drum. He enjoyed blowing the tailpipe, on which he was a master.

The tailpipe, which was really an exhaust pipe from a car, had to be properly cleaned, treated, and cured. You put hot sand in it and bent it into shape, so that the sound may flow. Next you poured sweet oil in it and let it set awhile. Only then it was ready for the pipe man's lips.

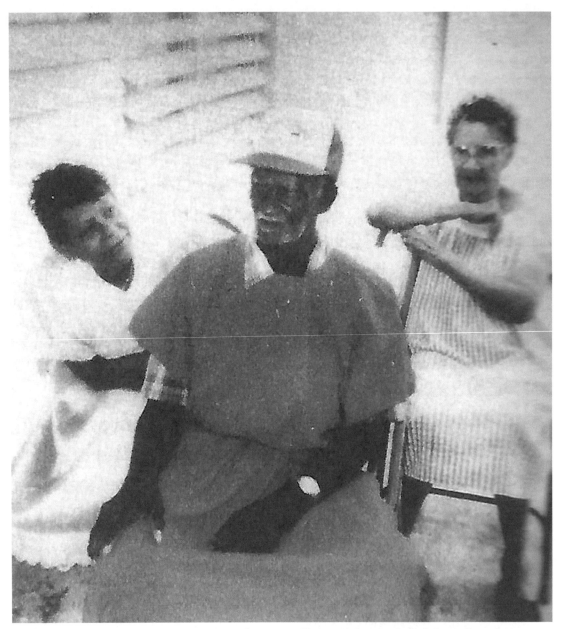

*Paddy Moore in a burlap sack at Whim Gardens. He was disappointed that a band was not going to play for his performance.*
*Photo by Luz Minerva and Noemi Osorio*        *Courtesy of Richard Schrader, Sr.*

Mr. Frankie Petersen described an unfortunate incident that occurred while Paddy Moore was masquerading. "One day while dancing in the street, dressed in his bulrush (banana leaves) costume, a man lit a match and set him on fire. Paddy ran to the sea on Strand Street and threw himself in the water. Luckily the burns were not severe."

Describing Paddy Moore, Frankie Petersen explained, "Paddy was a master masquerader and pipe man. He lived for many years in Santo Domingo and spoke fluent Spanish. He was over 90 years when he died in February 1995.

Regarding Albert Halliday, Frankie Petersen spoke about his street performances:

> He was another great performer who loved to sing, dance, and tell stories. One of his favorite pieces was "Tanto Liza." He also liked to pretend he was reading from a book, a ledger or Sears Roebuck catalog. As the calypsonians did with their songs, he too did with his make-up speeches. He didn't call any names, but everyone knew who he was talking about. He told humorous tales about politicians and other government officials. Some people were afraid of him because if they did anything out of the way, when the holidays came around Albert Halliday would make a speech about it and everyone would know.

Frankie Petersen reminisced about another street performer. "Isaiah "Marshall" Sealey who masqueraded as a mocko jumbie and also performed as one of the leading players in the David and Goliath groups. Marshall was a fisherman who mainly caught lobsters in Frederiksted, would boil them and carry them on a tray selling them throughout the town."

Frank Charles, in *The Glory Days of Frederiksted*, stated that he played music for some of the best masqueraders, including Paddy Moore and Marshall. He played banjo for Paddy Moore and drum for Marshall, the Mocko Jumbie. Mr. Charles described masquerading with Marshall:

At Christmas we'd start around eight in the morning and perform in different villages. Then around 3:00 p.m. we'd go to town and play until 6:00 p.m. That was a long day. Sometimes Marshall would take off his stilts to rest or he'd simply lean on a tree.

*A mocko jumbie performing in Frederiksted, early 1900s.*
*Photo by Axel Ovesen*         *St. Croix Landmarks Society*

*A mocko jumbie dancing on Market Street in Frederiksted,*
*early 1900s.*
*Photo by Axel Ovesen          St. Croix Landmarks Society*

Eulalie Rivera in her book, *Growing Up on St. Croix*, wrote about her encounter with a masquerader dressed as a Devil and while trying to run away her foot got caught in a fence at the Ebenezer Home for Children in Frederiksted. The Devil lashed her with a whip, which she described as "just a thin piece of stick ornately decorated." This story is also told on the *Zoop, Zoop, Zoop* recording compiled by music ethnologist Mary Jane Soule.

Mrs. Rivera explained the custom of collecting monies from the onlookers. She wrote, "I think the money they collected helped to pay for their costumes, some of which were quite elaborate. One member of the masquerade troop was responsible for collecting the money, and no matter which masquerader picked up the money, it was always given to the designated person. Later the money would be divided up among the musicians and members of the troop."

George Henry, in the book *The Sugar Industry on St. Croix*, spoke about the masquerades. "I was a country boy and the only other time besides going to school was to come to town to see the masquerades. Marshall, a Barbadian, was the first man to dance on stilts. He used to sell lobsters and he would get them from in the caves. He would walk around with a tray of lobsters on his head and shout, "The vagabond passing."

Gerard "Jerry" Doward, who grew up in Frederiksted, remembered the Wild Indian masqueraders performing on Strand Street where he lived when he was about eight or nine years old:

> On holidays the masqueraders, about five of them, would come up Strand Street towards Marley Homes. The masqueraders dressed with a headpiece having long peacock feathers and they had on some ugly-looking wire masks on their faces. I couldn't see their faces so I didn't know who they were. They had on a skirt-like outfit, long sleeve shirts, long beige color women stockings and worn out black and white high-topped sneakers. The skirts were about knee length covered with trinkets like glitter stuff and tiny round glass mirrors and were regular cloth material but different colors. They carried a grayish-color hatchet and one of them had a donkey costume made out of cardboard but well decorated.
>
> They danced jumping up and down and would swing the hatchet like they were going to hit you with it. They never said a word so you did not know what they

were going to do to you. Whenever they saw a child they ran after that child to frighten him or her. I remember a masquerader chasing one of my friends through the yard behind the outhouse. My friend got away and was not caught. It was mostly children in the street and a few adults looking on or looking out of their jalousie windows.

The masqueraders certainly frightened me. I would run to my godparents' house and hide under their bed and wouldn't come out until I heard the music going up the hill by Fisher Street. I heard the drum and flute music going up the street and that's when I would come out of the house. You would hear the flute, the bass drum which had a "bom" beat, the squash and the steel. The snare drum would have a rolling beat. I did not know who the musicians or the masqueraders were. The musicians were not masked but I did not know who they were. There were fungi bands and scratch bands but I don't know the difference. The masqueraders danced in front of the band with the musicians behind them. They probably went down King Street to perform. I don't know if the masqueraders and musicians I saw were from Frederiksted town or the country.

I saw Paddy Moore dance without a costume in his usual khaki clothes. All he needed to hear was a bass drum and he started dancing. Every Friday night he was in Percy Gardine Theater where First Bank is today. He sat in the general entrance section right in front of the screen. The movies started with The Big Picture, cowboys, super heroes like Captain Marvel, and World War II movies with the Japanese. I think the general entrance cost 25 cents while the reserved section was 35 cents.

Cherra Heyliger in a *St. Croix Avis* newspaper article about Christmas on St. Croix described the preparation for the festive season. He wrote, "Masquerades coming out" was the watchword. The tamarind whips were carefully covered. The wire masks with their frightening look were prepared and hung on the partition. The Mother Hubbard outfits were getting the final touches."

Mr. Heyliger further revealed the preparation of some popular street performers. He explained, "Back up many moons Christmas time on St. Croix meant the rehearsal of David and Goliath out in Golden Grove and Castle. Rehearsal of "Wild Indians" at La Grange Village, "Harden," Wheel of Fortune and even over to Prosperity pasture and William Pasture. By this time Frank Charles had finished and cured the skins of the best ram goats and they were ready to be stretched across small, medium and large kegs, and sometimes small barrels, and made into drums. The drum known as the "Kettle drum" was usually thin and so constructed that it brought forth high pitches which could be heard miles away."

Cherrra wrote of another great street performer who delighted the crowd and scared young children. "Marshall had caught his share of lobsters and it was time for him to play Mocko Jumbie, flashing his fineries with frilled bag drawers. What a spectacle as he hopped, danced and pranced on his ten foot stilts."

Eulalie Rivera, from Frederiksted, remembers Marshall, who was from Barbados, as the first person she saw on stilts. "No one could dive conch and lobster better than him. He sold three conchs for seven cents and lobsters that were already boiled. Taylor was another mocko jumbie and he used to wear skirts."

Dimitri Copemann's list of Frederiksted masqueraders and musicians includes Alberta Malone, Nellie Scott, Anna Mills, Augustina Nichols, "Bongo" Wallace, Payne, Cecil Brannigan, Kiah Braffith, Francis "Lime" Jack Edwards and Rosalia Bones.

# LIONEL "FIX ME" HUNTT

# Wild Indian Masquerader

Lionel "Fix Me" Huntt was born on May 7, 1898, in Christiansted and was a member of the Friedensthal Moravian Church. He was a mason by profession, but on holidays such as Easter Monday, Whit Monday, Fourth of July and Christmas Second Day he performed as a Wild Indian masquerader throughout the streets of Christiansted town.

His daughter Roselyn Huntt Galloway recalls that his theme was the Wild Indian. She remembers he used to go down the streets by himself not with a group. "His costume was a crocus bag with little round mirrors sewed on it and there were lots of mirrors. He wore long thick stocking hose up to his knees and had sneakers."

Winnifred Canton remembers her mother Octavia Huntt saying that Lionel danced on all the holidays, even the Fourth of July. Winnifred explained, "He dressed up and danced for fun. When the holidays were coming up he got ready. He also got the people who would play music for him. Maybe he went down the streets from 10 o' clock in the morning."

Yvonne Huntt Liburd, Lionel Huntt's daughter, reminisce that as a young girl she danced with her father on holidays. "I was about eight years old in the 1950s and I wore an old dress that I cut up. I carried an aluminum cup in my hands and picked up the money people threw on the street. I collected the money and gave the cup to my father. He counted the money which I never did since I was little."

Yvonne recalls how her father dressed up to masquerade. "My father had on a crocus bag with strips and mirrors. He wore a wire mesh mask and had Indian feathers in his hat. One time he had a cardboard donkey for his costume. A scratch band played the music for his performances. Ciple had a band with instruments made from lard and sardine pans. We performed from Watergut to King Street and at No. 22-C Company Street where I remember Miss Sigrid Rodriquez looking out her window."

*A Crucian Indian with long feathers dancing in front of spectators.*
*Photo by Fritz Henle     St. Croix Festival Booklet     Fair Use*

*An unidentified Wild Indian dancing and jumping up at Parade Ground in Christiansted, St. Croix, circa mid-1950s.*
*Photo by Fritz Henle        St. Croix Festival Booklet        Fair Use*

Yvonne consulted with her older sisters who reminded her that their father performed close to the Christiansted Saturday Market on Company Street because the merchants and several families who lived in two-story buildings were on that street. "Besides Miss Sigrid Rodriquez, merchants such as Antonio "Sundial" Gonzales and Clara Aloyo for Clara's Market threw money from their windows. The Pedersens also threw money from their window."

The sisters stated that their father was the first to make Fraico before Mr. Graham who sold his icy delights from a cart. Lionel Huntt had a little café shop in Watergut across from Valmy Thomas and next to the Romneys. There he sold sandwiches, fraicos, candy, and chicklets. He got the nickname "Fix Me" because customers would tell him what they wanted, and he would say "fix me" to them. Mrs. Octavia Huntt even ended up with her husband's nickname.

Yvonne explains how her sisters helped their father with the Fraico process. "Winnifred, Claudia and Elaine boiled the essence with sugar and their father made different flavors. Then he got blocks of ice, shaved the ice and poured the syrup over it to make the fraico. She remembers the flavors sold by her father. "The red strawberry was the most famous flavor for the fraico. He sold fraico made from local fruits such as pineapple and tamarind. The fraico was sold for 25 cents in little white cups."

Winifred noted, "He also made raspberry, guava and almond fraicos. Sometimes people wanted milk on their almond fraico so he poured milk on the top."

Christian Frorup, who lived in Watergut for many years, shared his recollection of Mr. Huntt. Frorup said, "Besides his shop he had a little taxi business on the side. When I worked at VICORP, the Virgin Islands Corporation that managed sugar cane production, the workers had to provide their own transportation. So about five or six of us got Mr. Huntt to drive us to Estate Golden Grove and back to Christiansted. He had a Ford station wagon, which I think was green and we paid him $5.00 every week for every one of us. He drove me for two years and this was back in the mid-fifties. Huntt was a very quiet man who I have never seen get mad yet. I stopped by his shop, which was in Watergut, by the Mirandas and across the street from Leocadio Camacho and Henry Williams. I bought ice, fraico, beverage and sometimes a beer. You could get a little liquor like a shot of whisky or rum from him. Tamarind was my favorite fraico. He even had candy jars on his counter. I mostly bought loose ice from his shop, and

*Wild Indians performing in a Festival Parade by the Lord God of Sabaoth Lutheran Church on King Street in Christiansted.*
*Photo by Egil Klint*          *St. Croix Christmas Festival Booklet*          *Fair Use*

you had to walk with your own container because the ice didn't come in bags like today. My family had a refrigerator, but we went to him for ice when we had a party."

When Mr. Frorup was asked if he knew Mr. Huntt used to masquerade his response was, "I didn't know he used to masquerade."

Mrs. Merle Finley remembers that "Fix Me" Huntt had a café and because drinks were sold her mother didn't want her to go inside. "We stayed outside and called our father Leopold Christian Derricks for anything we wanted inside. They played dominos there and played music. My father used to go there to play music with his guitar. Maude Andrews also played the guitar and Mr. Miranda played the steel. Sanna used to be there too. I didn't know "Fix Me" used to masquerade because they had on masks."

Roselyn H. Galloway spoke about her father Lionel Huntt's work as a mason. "He used cement and worked on the second half of the windmill by the Comanche. He died at 41 or 42 years of age when Comanche Hotel had moved across the street."

# VIGGO ROBERTS

## Masquerader

Viggo Roberts grew up in the King's Alley area of Christiansted in a long row that is now a bar. He was the son of Ruth Samuel Roberts, a cook who made sweet bread. Randall James, Viggo's grandson, remembers visiting his great grandmother on Sundays and sitting on a box outside the long row. Randall has fond memories of his grandfather Viggo and spoke of his participation in masquerading on the streets of Christiansted town and performing in several St. Croix Christmas Festival Parades.

"Viggo was a fisherman in Watergut even though he lived in Gallows Bay. His grandsons, along with their uncle, went with him to assist with the day's catch. We went to help him pick the mast by Holger Danske and had to row the bateau. We set the fish pot where the Seaplane is located today. Viggo also worked at Bethlehem with the sugar.

We had to follow him on all holidays that came up like Whit Monday and we played a different character each time. We went around town and children knew to run and hide under their beds. The characters we played were Wild Indians, Clowns and Zulus with machetes and pitchforks. Viggo has played the Ghost and the Bull, and I think he also used to do mocko jumbie.

His Wild Indian costume had a hat with peacock feathers and his pants was like Davy Crockett with different sequins. Some of the costumes were made by my uncle's wife Anna Jubie. She lived across from Merrill's Drugstore on Company Street. My cousin Eugene David also made some costumes for us.

Earl Jackson danced with the Wild Indians. Alma Christian and Cynthie James were sponsors. We won a first place prize in the 1960 Christmas Festival Parade and I think in 1961, too.

Viggo's Ghost costume consisted of a white sheet with holes cut out for eyes. Whatever Viggo chose to do he made sure that everybody had a costume. We practiced by the library where the Social Service office was located.

As Zulus in the Festival Parades, we dressed in a white diaper-like clothing and put black tar on our faces and all over our bodies. Viggo made a donkey for the February 22$^{nd}$ Washington's Birthday Donkey Races where he stood inside a barrel and danced.

Viggo was accompanied by musicians such as "Fonsa Knockout," a flute player, Gracie Ferdie's sister Anna played the squash and Randy Rawlins' mother. Alexander Williams, who used to hit the kettle drum, was nicknamed "Spotted Lamb" because he had lotta spots all over his body.

Viggo died when I was in either the eighth or ninth grade. That was before I went to the Central High School which opened in 1967."

Randall James grew up in Gallows Bay and in 1963, his family were among the first people to move to the Ralph de Chabert Housing Project. He left St. Croix to study journalism. His studies took him to Wisconsin, Maryland and New York and he worked as an X-Ray technician in New York City for many years. "Randy Pate," as he is called by many Crucians, is a frequent call-in guest on local radio talk shows.

Doreen Rissing Hay, from Christiansted, fondly remembers dancing with Viggo:

> I danced with Viggo in a Rhumba troupe and we went to different senior places and danced on certain holidays. Then, when Viggo came back to Christiansted he would dress up as a ghost harassing the children in the afternoon. Sometimes he dressed as a bull.

*Viggo Roberts in Pentheny Yard where today the King's Alley is located.*
*Courtesy of Randall "Pate" James*

Viggo took the Rhumba troupe over to St. Thomas on a boat in 1952, for that island's first Carnival. The boat was rocking and I got an upset stomach. So I told them I am going back to St. Croix on a plane, which is what I later did. We stayed by Gurline Gibbs, because Viggo was her uncle. The food they gave me helped my stomach and we had a good time over there.

Mildred Rissing Knight, from Christiansted, danced masquerade and also performed in troupes with Viggo.

I danced masquerade along with my sister Doreen, Maude King's mother Edith, and Gurline Gibbs, Viggo's niece. We lived in Pentheny Yard in a wooden long row house. Viggo, his brother Ivan Roberts and their mother Ruth Samuel lived there also and we practiced masquerade at night in that yard. Viggo could ah dance. When we danced masquerade we used to get money from people and when we finished performing we went by the well in Pentheny Yard to count the money.

Ivan Roberts used to play a guitar out of this world. Ciple played music with his biscuit pan and One Hand Dan played the long pipe. Ciple also played the long pipe and used to sing, "Mama no pue." We used to have fun. They played for us when we masqueraded in the streets.

When Viggo masquerade alone he would run people with his ugly costumes. And he coulda run fast. He hid his costumes and we never saw him get dressed or when he took off his costume. Not just children but big women running from him. I remember one holiday I had just bought some peanuts from Miss Martin who sold under Hamilton House gallery. Viggo came up the alley and scared me so that I dropped the peanuts and ran home.

Viggo, the troupe leader, used to have different troupes and I remember a Rhumba troupe with costumes having big sleeves and skirts with ruffles showing my legs. I loved to dance and people used to say, "Watch that one." Miss Florence Forbes, my godmother, sewed my costume. She used to sew for people and she used the

*Alexander "Ciple" Michael singing while hitting a kerosene pan.*
*Photo by Fritz Henle*                    *Fritz Henle Estate*

*Viggo Roberts dressed as a Zulu directing a children's Wild Indian Troupe on Company Street in Christiansted. Randall "Randy Pate" James is the third child on the left in this 1960 poster.*
*Courtesy of The St. Croix Landmarks Society*

*A bat with large wings in a parade possibly in St. Thomas.*
*Photo from Will Thurland Film Collection*

left over material for my outfit. She bought the sewing material from Claudina's Store on Queen Street in Christiansted.

Mrs. Mildred Knight concluded her thoughts on festival and dancing, "One year we had a troupe of all flags and people gave us money. I had loved to dance and my mother and father used to go to dances at the Congressional Hall on Church Street."

Ingrid Hendricks Bermudez remembers Viggo and his masquerading skits:

Viggo used to have the last troupe to come down the street, his Wild Indians. I was afraid because they had machetes and cutlasses. He used crocus bags for his costumes and had peacock feathers in his hat. A woman called "Sue Devil" used to dance with the troupe. On holidays Viggo came out by himself. He came down the hill from Canegata to the gut scaring everyone. You heard an echo in that gut by the Barracks Yard. Then, he went through Gallows Bay and on to Watergut. One year, I saw him dressed as a Bat. People used to give him money.

# ASTA WILLIAMS

## Masquerader and Culture Bearer

Asta Williams is very passionate about Virgin Islands history and culture, especially that of St. Croix. This culture bearer has dedicated her life to preserving the art of masquerading, making face masks and storytelling.

Asta Williams described her family's involvement and her subsequent interest in masquerading. "I was born in Estate Concordia across from Estate Good Hope and it was an Easter Monday. I remember a lot because my family was in masquerading. Both my aunt and grandmother were dancers. My father played the ukulele, banjo and a guitar that used to talk. He played music and went from estate to estate entertaining the people who lived in the villages.

On holidays we children didn't want to go out, you know, because of Marshall, the mocko jumbie, and Braffith, the Wild Indian. They went down all the streets of Frederiksted and up the hills looking for bad children. Years ago, people didn't call the police but they told the masqueraders. Parents would say, "Wait til the Mocko Jumbie come." One of the Mocko Jumbies used to come in the house even if you hid under the bed and he would grin at you.

Both Marshall and Braffith were fishermen and were strong dancers. The way they danced frightened children. Early in the morning before the sun came up you would see them. People were afraid because sometimes they come in your house. People didn't lock their doors back then.

I can see them now in their costumes. They dressed mostly with mirrors, their faces painted and wore a wire mask. When they had on their masks you didn't know who they were. They even made their own costumes. Those men were the only two Mocko Jumbies in Frederiksted. They didn't dance together and went dancing on different streets. I had liked to hear the drum beat that was played for their performances.

Any children they see on the streets, those mocko jumbies could ah run fast and come and dance in front of them. They had some scary moves. I had a cousin who lived on King Street in Frederiksted and she had an aunt called Nen, who she was going to visit and lived in a two story building. She darted across the street when she saw a mocko jumbie coming down the street. She locked the bottom door and went upstairs. As she got up the stairs and looked at the open window there was a mocko jumbie sitting on the window. Upon seeing him she passed out.

We had Mother Hubbard troupes. Charles Farrell's grandmother Nelly Scott's troupe dressed in clothes that imitated the "Misses" who lived in the Great House on the estates. I used to dance with Nelly Scott. There is a display at the Whim Museum with a dress and hat that my mother wore in one of those troupes. My mother used to like masquerades, especially the Cane Cutters troupe. I was about 14 years old when I participated in that troupe.

My mother dragged me along and we wore madras skirts and had whips. There were cane cutters and flower girls in the troupe.

You never saw masqueraders dressing or putting on their masks. They would go down a side street or go into someone's house where there were no children. They would walk with their costume inside a cloth bundle. She was active in the Bright Hour Circle and the Unity Club that were under the leadership of Mrs. Anita Christian."

A story in the book, *Quadrille: The Official Dance of the U.S. Virgin Islands*, states that Mrs. Anita Christian started the Bright Hour Circle in 1945 as a social club for the purpose of helping needy people. In order to raise funds, the organization held cultural dances, Tea Parties, Quadrille Dances, Formal Balls and Masquerade Dances.

*Field workers performing for the crowds in a 1962 Festival troupe in Frederiksted, St. Croix. Alma Doward has the basket on her head and Matilda Williams has a hoe.*
*Photo by Axel Ovesen*          *Courtesy of Gerard Doward*

*The Unity Social Club Festival Troupe on Fisher Street in Frederiksted.*
*Photo by Axel Ovesen*             *St. Croix Landmarks Society*

Asta Williams and the West End Masqueraders in a Festival Parade in Frederiksted.

*Photo by Gerard Doward*

"I remember hearing about a lady who danced masquerade and dressed in another lady's house. She went home after performing and had not taken off her mask. Her children saw this costumed person come into the house and got frightened. They ran and hid under the bed. She had to call out to them, "Tis me, Mommy.""

The first time I, by myself, saw a masquerader up close was when I lived in Christiansted. I lived in Watergut and walked up the street and sat by where the Bank of Nova Scotia was located on the corner of King and Prince Streets. A drummer and fife player were coming down the street. I sat with my daughter and was waiting for the parade to come down the street. When I looked up I saw this thing dressed in a white sheet. I thought it was a ghost with two eyes and it was very scary. I nearly passed out and there was hardly anyone on the streets. I froze and couldn't run because it might run after me. I think it was Viggo who had scared me.

Years later Sharon Browne danced masquerade with me. Sharon had a David and Goliath troupe which was based on the biblical story. My uncle, who was short in size, played David and Sharon's father was Goliath. They had the drum beat and performed for hours.

When I started masquerading the group met in a secluded place and we came out dressed in our costumes. Also, no one sees us undressing. We masqueraded at Harbor Nights in Frederiksted and hid to put on our clothes. We scared a lot of people. We sat in our Pitchy Patchy costumes at the wall by the hospital on Strand Street and never answered anyone who called out to us. One night we were sitting at the Old Poor Yard and were dressing and a boy and girl came up to us. The boy saw us and ran away leaving the girl behind.

I got started doing Pitchy Patchy through Amy Petersen Joseph. She had a Pitchy Patchy troupe for a parade. You don't go and buy fancy clothes for this troupe. You used what you have because the troupe depicted poor people. Even though you were poor you still had fun and enjoyed yourselves. We grew up poor and made the best of it. Cinderella Dress Shop in Frederiksted gave me some cloth and we made strips. Amy took an old long sleeve shirt and sewed on the long strips of cloth. You can glue on the strips but the sewing holds better.

Something happened with Amy's foot and I carried on with the masqueraders group. I started the West End Masqueraders. Now I have a foot problem and sometimes ride in a truck. I have been dancing in parades for over 30 something years. I play music with Bully Petersen and the Kafooners now.

On the parade route we drink water and juice, eat oranges or tangerines to put liquid back into our body. One year I passed out by Pond Bridge. The costume is heavy and you also have on a mask. Carl Christopher told me, "Drink water and you will sweat it out." I am very thankful for him giving me that advice.

When we dance we have to look out for each other. We had to be cautious especially at Harbor Nights. We dance as partners and dance with sticks and whips. You can't see to the side because of the mask and there are wicked people. Sometimes people throw popcorn at you to see if you can see through the masks.

One year I made a Bull costume with horns for my grandson and coming down King Street by the Lost Dog Pub in Frederiksted this big man came and ram his head into my grandson's stomach. My grandson flipped over and prevented himself from falling down on the street. He could have gotten injured if he did not break his fall.

Another time going down that same street, by the same establishment, a heavy set fellow held on to my stick and would not lose it. He was pulling on the stick and pulling me too. Some masqueraders came and ran him off with their sticks and whips by dancing around him. Similarly, on King Street, by the bakery, I told a man to move and he said, "I bet I throw this beer on you." So now I carry a stick with me all the time.

I use safe wire for masquerade masks but not for children. Safe wire is like a needle and can stick you. For them I use a softy, softy wire. We get masking tape if we want children to work with wire masks and we put cloth on the mask.

Older people used wire masks but I came up with the idea of making a soft mesh one. I do demonstrations at a lot of places, especially schools. I use a small glue gun when making masks while long ago people used a big eye needle and thread. Also, I use red paint for the mouth and black and white paint for the eyes.

I have trained others, both adults and youngsters, to dance masquerade. Some young girls want to wear short pants, almost nothing, so you need older people to perform. I have children who will carry on when I am gone. One or two will go down the street performing as masqueraders. Masquerading, it is telling a story. It is an African tradition and we protect villagers from sickness. Masqueraders also protect the parade just like the mocko jumbies.

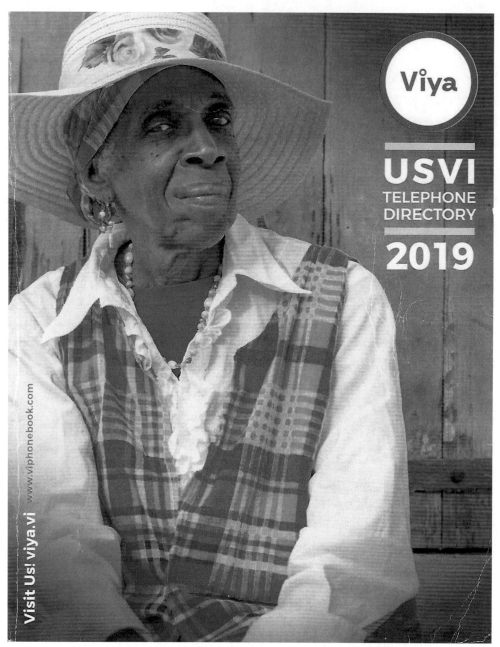

*Asta Williams on the cover of the 2019 Viya Telephone Book.*
*Photo by Stephanie "Chalana" Brown*        *Viya Telephone*

*Spectators viewing a Festival Parade on Fisher Street in Frederiksted. Notice the young boy in a cowboy costume with a gun and holster. Western outfits and guns with pop shots were Christmas gifts for boys back in the 1950s.*
*Photo by Axel Ovesen*                                                        *St. Croix Landmarks Society*

I was the Parade Marshall in the January 2019 Adult's Parade which was the last parade before the corona virus pandemic. The West End Masqueraders mixed together with the John Bull and Chalana Brown's troupe for that parade. For the next parade I will go on a float."

Asta Williams conducts classes in mask making and did tours with CHANT (Crucian Heritage and Nature Tourism). She is featured on the cover of the 2019 Viya Telephone Book dressed in madras. Also, Asta's face is painted on a mural at the Claude O' Markoe School's entrance in Frederiksted.

Ms. Williams can be seen on YouTube in a TV2 2019 production entitled *Virgin Islands Masquerading Traditions*. She is honored as a griot, one who passes on the oral tradition and customs of her people.

The St. Croix Landmarks Society has a Masquerade exhibit with costumes and masks made by Asta Williams. There are also pictures of Asta dressed as a masquerader along with such musical instruments as a tambourine, steel and a small drum.

# ERNEST "MIGHTY PRINCE" GALLOWAY

# Calypsonian

Ernest "Prince" Galloway from Watergut in Christiansted is a calypsonian known all over the Caribbean, the United States and Canada. He is unique for the fact that he is the only Virgin Islander who performed in Carnegie Hall in New York City and has been inducted into the Calypso Hall of Fame.

Ernest Galloway lived in Watergut as a young boy and attended St. Mary's School for a few years and then went to the Christiansted Public Grammar School, today the Florence Williams Public Library. He went on to the high school by the Barracks Yard.

Ernest remembers his Watergut neighbors. "We lived in the yard next to Miss Theodora Dunbavin. Then you had Alvin White and Nandi who had a boat in Gallows Bay and he had built a boat for the Comanche Hotel. He was family to the Bright Thirteen who lived on Hospital Street. Also living in Watergut were the Frorups, Peter "Boss Pete" Jackson, the Mirandas, Watson, Messer, Alexander "Popeye" Williams, Huntt for the laundry, Finley, and Thompson in the Grove. Wally "Whitey Pehe" lived on the corner across from Cipriani Shop.

We had a good relationship with everyone in our neighborhood. We, as children, respected our elders. Ciple played music with his kerosene pan and being older had his ways about him around us children. He wouldn't talk to young people like me only to the older folks. The other musicians I remember are the Simmonds Brothers and Joe Knight.

As a young boy growing up I listened to singers on the radio. Lloyd "Boney" Thomas was my favorite. He sang songs like "Island Girl Audrey," "Pig Knuckles and Rice," both songs were written by Gustav Civil, "I Want to Settle Down" and "Ten Rum Bottles." When I went to New York, after I finished school and served in the Army, "Boney" Thomas and I became close friends.

Dances were held by Mr. Miranda and at "Fix Me" Huntt's place. We went up to Happy Hours Yard in Western Suburbs and Catholic School dances at St. Mary's Hall. People used to dress up for those dances.

My father left St. Croix in 1946 to pursue better economic opportunities and my mother in 1951 followed him. He was an auto mechanic in St. Croix and in New York City. My siblings and I lived with our uncle Herbert Hendricks in a house back of the convent on Hill Street in Christiansted. In 1953 or 54, my father sent for the four of us and we went to New York. At that time most Virgin Islanders lived in the Bronx or Harlem and I lived on Eagle Avenue and 3rd Avenue in the Bronx. I had to get in groove with the weather and attending school in New York. There were a few West Indians at Morris High School at 166 Street between Boston and Unity or Trinity Avenue. That school is still there today.

After graduation, I was drafted into the United States Army and received basic training at Fort Knox, Kentucky and Fort Jackson, South Carolina. I was sent to Fort Dix, New Jersey and then on to Germany. When my service was up I returned to New York and got employment at Lord and Taylor, the Colgate Palmolive Company and later worked at a hospital on 80th Street."

When asked to define the music he sings Galloway explains, "Calypso is a cultural art done by our ancestors. People would say it comes from Trinidad but calypso was done by our older ancestors.

The popular dance halls in New York City were the Park Palace, Hunt's Point in the 50s and 60s, Audubon Ballroom, Rockland Palace, Manhattan Center, Carver Ballroom, and The Central Ballroom. I sang with Pedrito Altieri at The Paladium.

I was introduced to the Trinidad calypso by a lady named Myra Alexander. I sang with Rupert "Lord Invader" Grant and Al Thomas. I was a chorus singer for him and Myra told him to take me because she saw a calypsonian in me. We sang for white folks. We sang for the record label Folkways Records owned by Mr. Asch."

Research shows that Folkways Records was originally the label of Folkways Records and Service Corporation which was founded in 1948 by Moses Asch and Marian Distler in New York City to document music, spoken word, and sounds from around the world.

"Lord Invader sang in Europe, but I was not with him on that tour. His biggest hit was "Rum and Coca Cola." He treated me well, but I branched off on my own. I got the nickname "Mighty Prince" from a fellow from St. Croix, Marie Perry's son Moncell Isaroon.

I played music on the boat rides on the Hudson River. I just sang and did not play any instrument. Many Virgin Islands groups sponsored those boat rides. The boat would leave 125th Street down by the pier and go on a day cruise to Bear Mountain. I sang with Claude Brewster, Bert Samuel, Sid "Sid Jo" Joseph, "Fats" Greene, Ohaldo Williams and Milo and the Kings

People carried their own food, rum and drinks. They would get a setup from the bar like beer, cokes, small drinks and ice. You couldn't let the bar people know that you were bringing in your own liquor. There were lots of food to eat like fried chicken and salt fish gundy. People called the band over for food and drinks.

I sang for many Virgin Islands dances and also did some dances for Jamaicans in New York City. In 1959, I sang in the Festival Village on St. Croix with the Motta Brothers and the Vibratones for the festival committee. I recorded on St. Croix with the Vibratones whose members were Henry "Skipeo" Thomas, his brother Edwin Thomas, Herbie Gaskin, Dr. Randall James, Herman "Green bug" Thompson, Vincent Benjamin and Sackey, a singer.

In 1958, I met Sparrow and took him to a dance at 110th Street at the Park Palace and Lord Nelson was singing there that night. In 1965, I came in second to Sparrow when I sang "Archie Buk Me Up" in the Festival Village in Frederiksted. I think my songs "Crompo Boy" and "Archie Buk Dem Up" were road marches on St. Croix.

Milo and the Kings wanted me to sing with the band in St. Thomas, but I was living in New York at that time. We recorded with Cab Records in New York.

I recorded with the Limey Record label with Ohaldo Williams, a musician from St. Croix, who played in New York City for many years. I used my wife Roselyn's nickname which is Rosie for the label called Rosie Records. I met her through friends from home. She was a nurse in New York. I did not know her when I lived on St. Croix."

Roselyn Huntt Galloway and Ernest have been married over 58 years. She met "Gallo" as she affectionately calls him in 1959 in New York City. "My sisters and I used to go to all the dances in New York, to all Gallo's dances and especially when Milo and the Kings came up from St. Thomas. I met him at a dance."

Prince Galloway said that his wife and family went along with his singing calypso. They encouraged him to compose and sing throughout the years.

Prince Galloway describes his singing experience in Calypso Tents in Trinidad during the Carnival season. "My first appearance in Trinidad was in 1970 and the first person that introduced me to the Calypso Tent was Lord Melody and also Stalin. My second appearance was with Carlton "Lord Blakie" Joseph and Hollis "Chalkdust" Liverpool. My third appearance was with Fred "Lord Composer" Mitchell who was a Calypso Tent manager.

The band leaders I recorded with in Trinidad were Leston Paul and I made the song "Hess Man" with Art De Coteau. The Trinidadian singers I sang with were Campanero, Cypher, Eisenhower, Percy and Striker. I sang with Lord Nelson and with King Derby on St. Croix.

Ernest "Prince" Galloway performing in a Calypso Tent in Trinidad.
Courtesy of Ernest Galloway

To say that I have a favorite song is hard because I composed so many songs. I think of "Bring Back De Bacooba," "Josie," "Crompo Boy," "Hess Man" and "Archie Buk Dem Up."

Prince Galloway had several popular songs throughout his career to include "Crompo Boy" 1960, "Loretta/The Wedding" 1962, "Wahbeen" 1963, "Annette" 1971, "Watergonians" 1981, "Bom-Bom PP" 1982, Hess Man", 1983.

*Ernest "Prince" Galloway on a record cover.*
*Courtesy of Ernest "Prince" Galloway*

Galloway remarked, "Lots of people think Archie Thomas wrote the song "Archie Buk Dem Up" but I am the composer of that song which I composed in 1965. The organization BMI made me aware that "Archie Buk Dem Up" was being played in Europe. That song or it's music has been recorded by Ron Berridge in Trinidad, the Merry Men from Barbados, and Fats Greene in New York City. Even a group in Canada tried to claim that song. That's why BMI is very important for composers and other musicians."

# ARCHIE BUCK MIH UP

Last Carnival we had ah wonderful time

Archie buck mih up

Archie buck mih up


Everybody was dancing shaking dey bodyline

Archie buck dem up

Archie buck dem up


Dey go be jamming down dih road on Festival Day

Archie buck we up

Archie buck we up


Dih music is sweet. Listen to mih Crucian home beat

Archie buck we up

Archie is ah big mashup


Don't go to Archie if you ain't feel okay

Archie buck mih up

Archie buck mih up


*Written by Ernest Galloway, Jr.*

Broadcast Music, Inc. (BMI) is a music and performing rights organization in the United States. BMI's website states that it "is the bridge between songwriters and the businesses and organizations that want to play music publicly."

Prince Galloway said, "Calypso went down when calypsonians sang against Harry Belafonte. He was not from Trinidad but popularized the music in the United States.

Calypso today is different. There is a difference. I try to listen to today's calypso, but the style is different to the vintage calypso. It has a good beat and a fast rhythm. No calypsonians made money like Marcel Montano has done."

Prince Galloway has received several honors in the Virgin Islands and on the United States mainland. In 2002, he received an award from the St. Thomas Carnival Committee. In 2004, the Freshwater Yankee Organization, comprised of Virgin Islanders living in New York City, honored him and he received a certificate from the New York State Assembly. On October 29, 2005, he was honored by the Caribbean Sunshine Awards Organization in New York City and was inducted into the Calypso Hall of Fame.

The Hall of Fame's booklet wrote this about Galloway:

> Ernest Galloway is known in the calypso world as Prince Galloway and was often described by Lord Pretender as "a true, true calypsonian." He has been performing since the early 1950s with other well-known calypsonians such as Melody, Destroyer, Invader, and Cristo. "Prince Galloway" is a prolific composer and has toured the Caribbean extensively. He has produced many albums in Trinidad and his fans would certainly remember his great hit of the 1960s, "Archie Buck Dem Up."

Ernest "Prince" Galloway is an accomplished musician who continues to write calypso music and also writes musical advertisements for local businesses. He is a proud Virgin Islander and one of our musical giants.

# DR. STANLEY JACOBS

## Culture Bearer and Quelbe Musician

D r. Stanley Jacobs and the Ten Sleepless Knights are the musical culture bearers of Virgin Islands music. The band is sought after to perform for Quadrille dances, parties and various cultural events such as festival parades, the Crucian Rican Tramp and other entertainment venues. They have been performing Quelbe music for over fifty years and are the musical ambassadors for the Virgin Islands.

Stanley Jacobs in a recent interview recalled his life with music and states that he is happy to continue playing music. "I was interested in music from a child and at six years of age an old man taught me to play the guitar; that was my first instrument. My brothers had the banjo and sardine pans and they went to the Hotel on the Cay to play and sing. The tourists threw coins like nickels at them.

I learned to play flute with Stanford Simmonds and ended up playing with his band The Simmonds Brothers. I first played steel and squash until Stanford showed me how to play the flute. Wilford Pedro at Herbert Grigg Home also showed me.

We play Quelbe music, that's what it's called now. But we just call it music. The term "Quelbe" was used as derogatory, low class. Now it is high class music.

I started to play music in parades in the early 1960s with The Simmonds Brothers. I never see the parades because I was in them.

The band, the Ten Sleepless Knights, got its name from an expression that Pierpont Petersen used to say. We used to tease each other and Pierpont would say, "Ayo better leave me alone because I had ten sleepless nights." He was referring to his ten children. It was Eldred "Edgie" Christian who came up with the name for the band.

Ivan "Mr. Dance" Boyce hired us to play music in the Christiansted Market. We were at Cramer's Park and went and played that evening. When asked what was the band's name we called ourselves the Vikings for that playout.

The original band members were Herman "Green Bug" Thompson, Christian "Te" Thompson, Eldred "Edgie" Christian, Warren "Spitter" Walcott on sax, Gustav "Pee Wee" Scott, Pierpont Petersen, the first guitar man, and me. Bobby and Larry Jacobs came afterwards.

The Ten Sleepless Knights did our first recording in 1970 and we did a set of quadrilles and the Bull Dog song. George "Bagoon" O' Reilly recorded us at WSTX Radio Station at the Miracle Mile location. We went to the station to play for his birthday which was around the same time in October as "Green Bug" and John Moore.

Our song, The Butcher and the Politician, was a big hit then. Me, "Edgie" and a bunch of us made it up at a party. The band never practiced we just used to play music. We used to hang out drinking, gambling, cooking, all kind of things. We had been in bands and when we were at the Ranch, "Darkie's Yard" on Queen Street, we had our instruments and we played music. The Trojans used to practice there too. That steel band started in Darkie's Yard on Queen Street. "Darkie" Thompson was "Green Bug" and "Te" Christian Thompson's father.

Now the band does rehearse. Tino Francis got us into doing that. Ohaldo Williams played with us. He had his own band and sat in with every band.

Jamesie used to play a guitar down in the country at Whim and Campo Rico. It was Dr. Randall James that recorded him and his group and that set him up.

We used the name Six Pack when we do presentations at school. The original Quelbe music instruments is six. The steel, squash, guitar, banjo, pipe and flute; that's the basic instrumentation. Sometimes, we have two guitars, two banjos and sometimes a tambourine. It was six of us and we drank plenty of beers, a six pack of beers so that's how that name came about.

We have performed just about every place on St. Croix. Also, in St. Thomas, St. John, Tortola, Virgin Gorda, Jost Von Dyke, Antigua, St. Kitts, Miami, Atlanta, New Orleans, New York, Washington, D.C., Denmark and Martinique. Somehow, we never performed in Trinidad or Barbados.

I like music and I like to play, and I feel good when I am playing music. We have been trying to interest others. We went into schools teaching quelbe music and at one time we taught at every elementary school on St. Croix. We did a full-blown program at the St. Croix Educational Complex with Valrica Bryson, the music teacher.

Some of those Complex students came out good. The Ten Sleepless Knights started a scholarship fund for students who are going to study music and they had to come back to St. Croix. One of the recipient Sasha Alexander plays the flute and is now a music teacher. Rice, another student, is away; them two came out good. At Claude O' Markoe School the fourth, fifth and sixth graders were good but it break up because of politics. It was a pleasure to see them play.

The Ten Sleepless Knights first played in the Christiansted Market for the Crucian Rican celebration, but it blew up into a tramp. The tramp now starts in the early morning from Bassin Triangle, down King Street, turn up Company Street and stops in the Christian Hendricks Market. I did not realize that it was so big. I watched it on a video that people showed me. People come to St. Croix just for that January Crucian Rican and All Ah We Tramp like they do for the annual Agricultural Fair."

Stanley related his knowledge of masquerading and the masqueraders he was familiar with as a young boy growing up in the Gallows Bay neighborhood of Christiansted. "I saw masquerades when I was small. The last masquerade was when I was approaching my teens. The first I remember as a baby in my mother's arms when we lived in Schjang Yard on Hospital Street.

There was a man with a cane bill frightening children. Parents used to warn their children, "Viggo coming after you."

The masqueraders came out in the afternoons on big holidays like Christmas Second Day, Whit Monday and the Fourth of July. A set of masqueraders and musicians with drum and steel would start up by English Church Hill, St. John's Anglican Church, come down King Street to Gallows Bay. When the man hit the bass drum, we heard it all the way down in Gallows Bay. I liked that drumbeat.

The Wild Indians came to Gallows Bay with "chaney" and glass bottles tied on to their costumes. Their faces were covered with a mask made from screen wire. You could not tell man from woman because of the long clothes and the masks.

Viggo Roberts, who lived across from me, was the star, jumping up and performing. He used to tease the children. Viggo had on something tight fitting like black leotards on his whole body and around his waist was something brown. He wore a mask or a crown. He used to frighten all ah we children. He used to jump up high in the air and swing the cane bill, mostly at the children. I last saw him in the early 50s when I must have been twelve or thirteen years old.

David and Goliath performances used to be done in Gallows Bay. I saw this guy we called "Tarzan" play Goliath and David was "Bull Head" Gerard. Goliath was dressed like a king with something on his head and a robe like a dress. David wore a pants and shirt and had a cloth with a rock stone in it. Somehow, "Bull Head" picked up a piece of 2 X 4 lumber and hit Tarzan with it. Tarzan stopped performing and ran after him.

Masqueraders used to be with them and there was music in between the talking. They used to stop to demonstrate at several homes and by Mr. White's Rum Shop.

Monroe Clendenen came with his pirates, and they performed. Also, the donkey in a half barrel with a head used to dance. The donkey costume was well decorated.

It had a lot of women, but you could not see any skin. The masqueraders covered their hands and legs with brownish, pinkish stockings and wore long dresses. You could not see no face, hand, foot, nothing. They all had chaney, glass bottles tied on to a crocus bag."

*Stanley Jacobs won the competition for the 1956 -1957 Festival booklet cover and received a $15.00 prize and told me that was a lot of money in those days.*

*Courtesy of Stanley Jacobs*

*Dr. Stanley Jacobs playing his flute at a function at Government House.*
*Photo by Karen C. Thurland*

*Stanley and the Ten Sleepless Knights entertaining the crowd at Cramer's Park for the annual Hillsiders Picnic. Left to right: Tino Francis, Dr. Olaf "Bronco" Hendricks, Gilbert Hendricks, Dr. Stanley Jacobs, Eldred "Edgie" Christian, Harold Johnson and Christian "Te" Thompson.*
*Photo by Karen C. Thurland*

The Virgin Islands community has shown its appreciation for the cultural contributions that Stanley Jacobs has made with his music. In 2017, the University of the Virgin Islands awarded him an honorary doctorate degree. The Festival Village at the 2019-2020 Crucian Christmas Festival was named "Stanleyville" in his honor.

In 2022, Stanley and the Ten Sleepless Knights instituted an Academy of Culture for all ages with Saturday sessions at the St. George Botanical Garden. The Academy offers a series of weekly activities based on the U.S. Virgin Islands culture and history and how they intertwine with our storytelling and the territory's official cultural music and dance. Instruction includes music, history, and Quadrille and masquerade dance.

On June 25 and June 26, 2022, the Ten Sleepless Knights held several cultural workshops at the Folklife Festival at Estate Whim Plantation Museum grounds. This year's theme was "Music, Dance, and a Cultural View." It featured storytelling, Moko Jumbies, Quadrille/Maypole dancing, Cariso singing and drumming, mask making, Crucian cooking demonstrations, Madras Head ties demonstrations, basket weaving and traditional Quelbe and masquerade music. The 2022 Folklife Festival held a program on July 3rd, commemorating the Emancipation of enslaved Africans in the Danish West Indies, providing a historical account of Emancipation, a Quelbe Tramp and a Quadrille Dance with the Ten Sleepless Knights.

The National Endowment for the Arts in continuing its long tradition of honoring America's rich artistic heritage selected Stanley Jacobs as a 2022 NEA National Heritage Fellowship recipient. National Endowment for the Arts Chair Maria Rosario Jackson, Ph.D. wrote, "In their artistic practice, the NEA National Heritage Fellows tell their own stories on their own terms. They pass their skills and knowledge to others through mentorship and teaching. These honorees are not only sustaining the cultural history of their art form and of their community, they are also enriching our nation as a whole."

Stanley Jacobs and his music will live on forever with the Ten Sleepless Knights musical recordings and the students who benefitted from the scholarship program and returned to the Virgin Islands to contribute to our musical and cultural legacy. Stanley Jacobs is a culture bearer and a musical icon in the Virgin Islands.

# THE OLD TIME ST. CROIX CHRISTMAS FESTIVAL

According to Harold Willocks, "It is not really known how the Christmas Festival really started. The first organized festival is said to have occurred during the final years of the Danish government before World War I. At that time, the festival was from December 26 through New Year's Day.

This organized festival was gradually abandoned. In 1952, the St. Croix Festival was revived through the efforts of the St. Croix Women's League, at the suggestion and urging of second vice-president Hilda England."

Yes, it was women who got the ball rolling with the St. Croix Christmas Festival. Mrs. Hilda Bastian England of the St. Croix Women's League suggested the revival of the old-time masquerades which were disappearing. In the summer of 1952, Mrs. England and Mrs. Anna Brodhurst, the President of the League, and several committee members planned a week-long festival which became known as the Old Time Christmas Festival and got the approval from David C. Canegata, the St. Croix Administrator.

Mrs. Anna Brodhurst in an interview with Diana Pearson for *The Daily News 1980 Special Edition* remarked, "The boys were coming home from Korea. We decided to have an old-fashioned Christmas." Mrs. Brodhurst remembered that masqueraders came out on Christmas Second Day and Three King's Day so activities were planned for those days. Mrs. Anna Brodhurst, Mrs. Hilda England, Mrs. Oran Roebuck, Mrs. Hephzibah Pretto Edwards, and Mrs. Elena Ovesen,

*Mrs. Anna Whitehead , wife of the publisher of the St. Croix Avis*
*and President of the Christiansted Women's League, was one of the*
*organizers of the Old Time Christmas Festivals.*
*St. Croix Mas Festival 1956 Booklet*         *Fair Use*

*Mrs. Hilda Bastian England, an elementary school teacher, counselor and*
*a member of the Third Constitutional Convention was instrumental in the*
*formation of the Old Time Christmas Festival. The Virgin Islands Board of*
*Education has established a scholarship in her name.*
*Painting by Elroy Simmonds*      *Courtesy of Carmen H. Simmonds*

of Christiansted, along with Mrs. Eulalie Rivera, second vice-president of the Frederiksted Women's League and Mrs. Beryl Armstrong made up the committee that first year, the 1952-53 Festival.

The Christiansted Women's League called their celebration, "Old Time Christmas Festival" while the Frederiksted Women's League, through Mrs. Eulalie Rivera, gave that year's festival the slogan "Kill Ting Pappy" which means "Have a good time."

In Christiansted, Christmas trees were put up in Gallows Bay, Watergut, Sunday Market, Free Gut, on the Wharf and at Bassin Triangle. In Frederiksted, cans were painted in bright colors and strung across the street.

Helen Joseph, a Festival troupe leader from Christiansted, in a *St. Croix Avis* article of December 15-16, 2002, by Cheyenne Harty provided insight into the lighting of the town streets. "I remember how school children peeled the paper labels from the cans and then strung them together like popcorn for a Christmas tree. The shiny aluminum cans would reflect the limited lights, making the town shine in silver."

A news article for *The Daily News 1980 Special Edition* by Diana Pearson stated that church bells all over St. Croix rang at 6 p.m. on Christmas Eve of 1952 signaling the opening of the festival. It furthered stated, "Christmas Day was for caroling and going to church. Christmas Second Day had masquerades in both towns, the lighting of the public Christmas tree followed by a lantern tramp, a quadrille the next day, more caroling and a parade on New Year's Day."

Parades were held in both Christiansted and Frederiksted. Mr. Monroe Clendenen, a goldsmith, stepped out as the first Grand Marshall of the parade in Christiansted, which was held on December 27th, while the parade in Frederiksted took place on New Year's Day. The parade entries had music provided by scratch bands and local orchestras.

Lito Valls, author of *What a Pistarckle! A Dictionary of Virgin Islands English Creole* and a historian with the National Park Service on St. John, was the editor for the 1952 Festival booklet. He explained how surprised he was at the community donations he received for the Festival. "I left my house on King Street, across from Government House, and walked up King Street to the Firm of John Alexander. By the time I got there I had collected $1,000.00 from businesses."

*Old Time Christmas Festival St. Croix Souvenir Booklet:*
*December 24, 1952 to January 1,1953.*
*Old Time Festival Souvenir Booklet*                    *Fair Use*

*A Cruzan Rum advertisement in an Old Time Christmas Festival Booklet. Cruzan Rum has been a loyal sponsor for the St. Croix Christmas Festivals since this annual event began in 1952.*
*Old Time Christmas Festival Souvenir Booklet          Fair Use*

The Christmas Festival Program for the 1952-1953 activities lists the ringing of all church bells and the sounding of sirens in Christiansted and Frederiksted at 6 p.m. to mark the official opening of the Festival and attendance at midnight church services in all Churches of both towns. The organizers did not want to interrupt religious Christmas services and this shows the importance of religion to our community back in the early 1950s.

The Festival Program included a breakdown of the dates and activities starting with Christmas Day and continuing until New Year's Day. Some of the events were caroling in the towns and country districts, Christmas Day services in all churches, masquerades on Christmas Second Day, a parade in Frederiksted, Community Christmas Tree lighting, and a Lantern Tramp, Quadrille Dance, ball games, Community Christmas Tree with Santa, Spanish and English singing groups, a musical concert on the Wharf by the Motta Brothers Orchestra, where Will Thurland, my father, played just as he did with that group of musicians for the first St. Thomas Carnival a few months earlier. Finally, on New Year's Day there were masquerades in both towns and the country districts. Then they headed to Christiansted for the parade that was scheduled for 2:00 p.m. The night ended with a Quadrille and Lancers dance with groups from both towns performing on the Basketball Court.

The General Committee for that first year consisted of the Chairman and Vice Chairman, Secretary, Treasurer, as well as committees such as Carols, Square Dances, Masquerading, Candy Collection, Soliciting Committee, Decoration, Parade, and Raffle Committee. The volunteer committees comprised of the Women League's members and outstanding people in the community, to include Annie de Chabert, Elena Christian, Eloise Moore, Gwendolyn Delemos, Wilhelm Samuel, Maria Thomas of the Bright Hour Circle, Rita L. Forbes, Pearl Thomas, Flora Blanchette, Jessica Dagget, Ejnar Bolling, Ignatius Jackson, A. Sebastian Forbes, C. J. Richards, Frank Petersen and Harry Kouch.

Some of the sponsors for the 1952- 1953 Christmas Festival booklet were Christiansted Utilities Company, Rasmussen's, Bloch Center, Jacob's Photo Shop, Club 16, Merrill's Apothecary, Carib Cellars, Sealey's Auto Repairs, The International Shop, Island Fancy Cleaners, Frederiksen's Drug Store, Virgin islands Tours, Rob'T L. Merwin & Co. Inc., Merwin's Ice Cream Parlor, Brodhurst's Printery, The Rubaiyat, L.M. Nielsen, Christiansted Theater, First and Last Stop Bar and Grocery, Ida Joseph's Dry Goods Store, Island Sport Shop, White's Bar, Square Deal

Printer, Cruzan Rum, Clemente Cintron, E. S. Crawford, Blanche's Taxi Service, Thurland's Cabinet Shop, Caribair, Christian Christiansen, St, Croix Laundry Company, Crucian Grocery, Popular Bar, St. Croix Beer Garden, Carter's Carpentry Shop, Eusebio's Bar, Dyer's Service Station, Rosedale Guest House, AyAy Shop and Bar, Bata, Santana's Taxi Service, Sky View, Cable and Wireless (West Indies) Ltd., Lionel A. Hendricks, Princess Night Club, Virgin Islands Beverages, Inc., The Cage, McFarlane & Company, Mademoiselle, Edna's Store, Jose Calderon, The Hide-A-Way Club, Abramson's Auto Service Center, Continental, Inc., Anduze's Barber Shop and Los Muchachos.

The Women's League again in 1953-1954, under the leadership of Mrs. Hilda England, the chairman from Christiansted, and Mrs. Eulalie Rivera of Frederiksted, the vice-chairman, organized the Festival activities for the Christmas festivities. The Steering Committee for that year's Festival had a few new committees. Besides the Chairman and Vice Chairman, there were the Corresponding, Treasury, Publicity, Decorating, Transportation, Dance, and Radio committees.

The 1953–1954 Christmas Festival Program gives us a view of the activities and again show the importance of religion in our community at that period of time. The events started out with religious services during Christmas Day and no events were scheduled to interfere with the church services. The pageants in both towns were held in the evening. Masqueraders came out from 3 p.m. until 6 p.m. on Boxing Day, Christmas Second Day, and both towns had a Lantern Tramp. The towns of Christiansted and Frederiksted had Lantern Tramps on their program schedule for December 29.

What were Lantern Parades or Tramps? Here are a few recollections about those night-time street gatherings that were held in both towns. My mother, Modesta Larsen Thurland, spoke often of my father Will Thurland going to the Lantern Parades and tramping down the street with the youngest child on his shoulders. As a young girl I remember being on my father's shoulders by Sunday Market and seeing the Chinese lanterns down the street.

Aurelia Cepeda Estrill lived in Christiansted on Market Street up from Alejo's and next to the Mottas. She recalled the Lantern Parades of the early fifties:

I used to look out the window and see people wearing old clothes and carrying lanterns going down to Sunday Market. Some people had a stick like a clothes line stick holding the lanterns. I think they lined up by Alexander Theater and went down King Street. It was mostly women involved in the parade. They had their own music, like someone beating a pan.

One year my mother, Elaine Forbes, and Mercedes "Cedes" Jackson had a Chinese troupe and I was in it. Both women worked at the hospital and planned that activity. I babysat the grandchildren for Mrs. Anna Brodurst while she, Cedes Jackson and a group of people planned what they were going to do for the parades.

Ingrid Hendricks Bermudez from Gallows Bay recalled, "The people for the Lantern Parades gathered at the Market and would tramp down to the village on the Wharf. A price was offered for the best lantern and many came from New York but some people made their own paper lanterns. A few times I have seen the lanterns catch afire because of the candle that was inside, so some lanterns were held on a stick."

Gerard Doward in *The Glory Days of Frederiksted* reminisced about the Lantern Parades in that town. "It was like a Chinese festival. There would be lanterns like the ones the Chinese use. It would take place at night and the beautiful colors would illuminate the evening sky."

Mr. Doward, in an interview further explained the Lantern Parades stating, "The Chinese lanterns were different colors, made of tissue paper and held on a stick. These lanterns were elongated with an opening at the top. The light was made by a small candle inside the lantern. The various groups made their own lanterns. The Lantern Parades were small parades that went down Queen Street in Frederiksted."

A historical account of the December 25, 1953 to January 1,1954, Old Time Christmas Festival is documented in the 1958 Festival Booklet:

In 1953, a new attraction was added. Lights were solicited on WIVI Radio station by G. Luz James and Felix Francis to decorate both towns and the public made a wonderful response. A 20-foot Christmas tree was installed on the Wharf in Christiansted, given by the Chamber of Commerce to the Festival, and some decorative bulbs were added by the Committee. This ran to almost $600, but with the help of the Jonkey Club, the Police Athletic Club and the Legislature, much was accomplished.

Two steel bands were invited from the British islands to play in the Festival. It was the first time that these bands had played in a festival parade in St. Croix. Hell's Gate Steel Band from Antigua played in Christiansted, and the Casa Blanca Steel Band from St. Kitts played in Frederiksted. The men were housed in vacant government buildings.

An account of the introduction of steel bands to St. Croix written in the 1956-57 Festival Booklet is as follows:

Mr. Brodhurst took them around the Island where the steel bands played free for the hospitals, institutions for the poor and inmates of the penitentiary. He found engagements for them at a few hotels and dancehalls, transported them to play, and let them keep the money they made. When they played at the Jungle Casino on Market Street (later the Crucian Moon and today the Boys and Girls Club of Christiansted) forty people went inside to hear them, while 500 stood outside, swearing that such strange instruments could not make the music that they heard. The St. Croix Avis announced that there would be a concert on the Wharf and three thousand people jammed the streets to listen. The band played for hours. Donations were collected and was so unexpectedly large that they were able to go home with the money for new instruments. When they departed for Antigua most of the island went to see them off and wish them a speedy return.

Several new sponsors for the 1953-1954 Christmas Festival booklet were Robert Armstrong Ford Dealer, Unity Corporation Dry Cleaners, St. Croix Memorial Company, Christiansted Auto Garage & Tire Shop, Hoffman's Variety Store, Chico's Bar & Pool Room, Tropicana, Pivar's Realty Company, Motta Bros. Record Center, Johnny Belardo's Grocery, Miquel's Grocery, Henry Joseph's Dry Goods Store, Berg's Garage, Nydia's Store, Anna Rijos, Basilio's,

Benjamin's Radio Service, Edna's Store, Philco, The Steadman Co. Inc., Cintron's Self-Service Grocery, Egil H. Klint, Hendrick's Butchery, Mencho's, Atti's Studio, Richmond Plantation House, Manocan's Pool Room and Bar, RCA Victor, The Fish Bowl, Reliable Furniture, Carlton Estate and Golf Club, Fabulous Fash Nite Club, Markoe Agencies, The Little Guard House, C. R. T. Brow, Claudina's, Rohlsen's Sales Company, Cruzana, Gomez Store, Simmond's Bus Service, Messer's Express & Hauling, Pink Fancy, Jones' Cocktail Lounge, Bough's Service Station, Fifo's Meat Market, St. Croix Sugarcane Industries, Inc., Julio Delgado Rucci, Caribe Lumber and Trading, Pedro Encarnacion's Barber Shop, I. Jackson's Grocery, Lammer's Bakery, The Hanover Fire Insurance Co. of New York, Mr. & Mrs. R. de Chabert, Stridiron's Guest House, Dr. & Mrs. Reginald Moore, and The Danish House.

The Women's League also organized the 1954 – 1955 Festival with Mrs. Hilda England in charge for Christiansted and Mrs. Beryl Armstrong for Frederiksted. That year the first King and Queen of the Christmas Festival were added, and they were Mr. Harry Edwards, a chemist from Watergut, and Miss Jessica Tutein from Gallows Bay.

Mrs. Jessica Tutein Moolenaar, in a *Daily News* interview, recalled being crowned the first Festival Queen because she and her King, Harry Edwards, sold the most tickets and raised the most money. Contenders that year were G. Luz James Sr. and O' Neal Henderson with their wives. It is important to note that Jessica's granddaughter Crystal Henderson was the first Hal Jackson's Talented Teen International winner from the Virgin Islands.

Ingrid Hendricks Bermudez, Jessica's daughter, recalled that her mother's dress for the event was made by Edris Clendenin McNamara and Henville Rogiers. She remembers hearing that they wanted something to positively uplift the spirits of the people so they formed the Festival.

The 1955 - 1956 Christmas Festival had two steel bands again invited from the British islands, plus two sets of clowns, The North Side Clowns from Antigua and the East End Clowns from St. Kitts. Additional information about the Festival in that year's booklet included the following:

> The Coronation Premiere was held in the Alexander Theater. Outstanding workers in the Festival were Mrs. Helena Ovesen, Mrs. Mary Andrews Phaire, Mrs. Beatrice Christensen, Mrs. Hilda England, Mrs. Pearl Thomas, Miss Ina James, and Mrs. Beryl

*Jessica Tutein and Harry Edwards, the first King and Queen for the St. Croix Festival, riding in a phaeton in a Festival Parade in Christiansted. Photo by Fritz Henle        St. Croix Festival Booklet        Fair Use*

Armstrong, who worked on committees of various kinds. Mrs. Alberta Miller, Miss Jessica Tutein, Mrs. Lillian Bailey, Miss Marie Edwards, Miss Viola White, and Mrs. Leola Carroll solicited for booklets and carolers. For decorations the workers were Mrs. Atti Henle, Mrs. Anita Dickerson, and Mrs. Ruth Gregory. In charge of Street Decorations were Ove Olsen, Henville Rogiers, Luz A. James, and Ignatius Jackson.

Wilhelm Samuel, Eddy Hendricks, Claude Richards, Aldin Benjamin, and none other than Alfred Ovesen handled all bingo games, etc., for the Festival. Bernadine Abramson, who donated his dance hall free, was a true "Leaguer." Eric Carroll was a Leaguer advisor, and Minard Jones and his friends made the lights for two streets.

The two parades were continued. Carols were sung in the early morning, and radio programs were given by various churches and school groups in keeping with the season. Church services were doubled, for never once were the festivities allowed to clash with the real meaning of Christmas. Guest houses and hotels filled as hundreds returned from the mainland to spend Christmas.

Nineteen hundred and fifty-five saw the Festival grow to such magnitude that the Christiansted Women's League thought it would be better to have many more groups handle it. So Mrs. Anna Brodhurst summoned a group to her aid, and they took over. The new attraction that year was a Festival Princess. Mr. J. O'Neil Henderson was in charge of the Parades and along with such men as Peter Christian and Attorney Frank Padilla of Frederiksted were able to put over one of the biggest parades ever to be seen in Frederiksted. The Women's League in Frederiksted, under Mrs. Christiansen, still continued to guide things there. That year, Miss Lydia Nico was the Festival Queen.

Several new sponsors for the 1955-1956 Christmas Festival booklet were Sylvia's Magazine Store, Marshall, Quin's Stationary & Novelty Store, Waite Construction Co., Charles L. Hilborn & Assoc, Inc., Treasure House, The Comanche, Dam's Liquor Store, Pedrito, St. Croix by the Sea, WIVI Radio Station, The Alexander Hamilton Supply and Hardware Store, Bruce Millar, Norbeth's Beauty Parlor, Santa Cruz Pharmacy, The Buccaneer, and The Firm of John Alexander.

*Lydia Nico, the St. Croix Festival Queen for 1955-1956.*
*Photo by Fritz Henle     St. Croix Festival Booklet     Fair Use*

Lydia Nico Thomas, the second Christmas Festival Queen for 1955-56, reminisced on her participation in Festival and other activities. Mrs. Anna Brodhurst had a youth committee for Festival where Lydia worked with advertising and she decided to run in the Queen's competition.

Lydia reminisced about her experience as Queen of the Christmas Festival:

> The contestants had to sell tickets, and who sold the most tickets won the popularity contest. It was a white paper book and you wrote the name of the person who bought the ticket so you would have an account of how many tickets you sold.

There was a show where all the participants modeled their dresses. I wore a beautiful white dress that I sewed with material and lining I got from Miss Sigrid's store. I also did my hair. At that time, I was seventeen years old.

On parade day I sat on a float decorated by the Committee and that activity started at the head of town led by the St. Croix Community Band and ended up at the Wharf where a stage had been built for the performances. On the stage there was a ceremony and then entertainment with dancers and music. The Simmonds Brothers and Ciple probably provided the music. A steel band, the Moonshiners, also played music. The members were the Llanos brothers, the Evans brothers and Bobby Skeoch, and I think one of my brothers and Harold Johnson also played with them. During my reign I went to the St. Thomas Carnival and to Puerto Rico representing St. Croix.

You can say that the spirit was embedded in me from young. I started dancing and performing when One Hand Dan came to our house masquerading. My father Nicasio Nico insisted that we dress up in old clothes and play music with biscuit pans.

I got my sewing skills from my mother who did a lot of sewing and she made Mrs. Anna Brodhurst's hats. She also sewed outfits for Mrs. Pretto, Mrs. Annie de Chabert, Mrs. Petrus and her close friend Mrs. Graham.

Lydia Nico Thomas was a registered nurse and head of the nurses' union. She married Valmy Thomas, a catcher for the Giants and the first Virgin Islander in the Major Leagues.

Additional information on the Moonshiners Steel Band was given by Mandy Llanos and Gerald Evans. Mandy Llanos shared his notes and photographs of the band and listed some of the activities they were involved in on St. Croix and even a playout on the island of Vieques, Puerto Rico:

The Moonshiners Steel Band originated in 1954 by Felix Llanos and Malcolm Evans and I was only twelve years of age when I joined them. Mandy was the

Captain and played lead pan. Our first playout was at St. Croix by the Sea Hotel. In 1959 we competed in the Christmas Pan competition and won with the "Hour Father" song. Our prize money was $25 dollars.

The pan yard was in Mr. Nicasio Nico's yard adjacent to the parking lot on Strand Street. Most of us were in the St. Mary's School Band and Glee Club and some were self-taught.

After that we had numerous play outs which include the Rubiat, Stone Balloon, Gentlemen of Jones, Fabulous Fash, King Christian, Comanche and many others. The band lasted for many years until members went to college or the Army. As of now, the only surviving members are Gerald Evans, Tommy Reynolds, Peter Flick, Johnny Encarnacion and myself.

Mr. Llanos also spoke of a girls' steel band. "There was also a girls' steel band named "The Bells of St. Mary's." Some of the members were Shirley de Chabert, Merely and Angela Christian, Aracelis Bermudez, Susan Wade and Lynette Lang."

Gerald Evans remembers his playing days with the Moonshiners Steel Band and how the band got started:

The Moonshiners got started in 1954 or 55, when the Hell Gates Steel Band from Antigua left St. Croix and they left some of their steel pans behind. They used to play in Mr. Nico's yard so there is where we practiced. A man called Raycan stayed on the island and he was one of the guys who taught us to play steel pan.

We played for Lantern Parades and ended up at the big tamarind tree by the Bandstand. The band have even gone on top of the cistern by the Christiansted Post Office where the dignitaries used to sit. The Moonshiners have even played music on the island of Vieques, Puerto Rico.

*The Moonshiners Steel Band from Christiansted.*
*Back row: Left to right, Johnny, Galo, Delray, Eugenio, Felix,*
*McAlpin, Peter, Andrew, Mandy and Malcolm. Front row: Left*
*to right, Rafa, Bobby and Elliott Nico.*
*Courtesy of Mandy Llanos*

The Festival booklet for 1958 described the continued growth of the Christmas Festival. "Nineteen hundred and fifty-six again saw Mrs. Brodhurst as the chairman of the Festival in Christiansted, and Mrs. Beatrice Christiansen again in Frederiksted. The new attraction was an invitation to the Carnival Queen from Puerto Rico, our own Festival Queen, Miss Mable Simmonds, and the Carnival Queen from St. Thomas. Singing and dancing were in order."

Mable Simmonds gladly shared her experience as a Festival Queen. She later married Allen Brady and together they ran the popular Brady's Restaurant, which sold Crucian food and was a meeting place for politicians. Mable said, "My classmates from St. Mary's School told me to run for Festival Queen. At that time, I was living with my aunt, Mrs. Annie de Chabert, across from where the medical building on Queen Street would later operate."

Mable described her winning the competition and she explained that who sold the most tickets won. She remembers the tickets were like a booklet with individual pieces that sold for 25 cents a-piece. Her sponsor was the de Chabert Dairies.

Mrs. Mable Simmonds Brady described the dress she wore as Festival Queen. "The dress I wore for the night of the crowning at St. Mary's Hall and in the parade was my cousin Rita's wedding dress. Only my aunt and I knew about that."

When asked about the parade, Mable said, "I was on a convertible car that took me from St. Mary's School to Company Street, Market Street and down King Street to the Christiansted Wharf. I went and sat with the other contestants on a stage that had been built for the festivities. The lady from C & M Boutique asked us questions about our age, hobbies and a few other things I can't remember. I was the oldest in the group. She did say that I was so pretty."

Mable concluded, "The music for the parade was provided by Archie Thomas, Ciple, and the Casa Blanca Steel Band from Frederiksted and the Hell's Gate Steel Band that was housed in Christiansted."

*Mable Simmonds, St. Croix Festival Queen 1956-1957.*
*Photo by Fritz Henle        St. Croix Festival Booklet        Fair Use*

The 1958 - 1959 Festival booklet article stated, "In 1957, the popular senator and radio announcer (Ron de Lugo) was chairman of the Festival with Ulric Benjamin as co-chairman, and they operated under the slogan, "Bigger and Better Each Year." This was the year that the Festival Village on the Wharf in Christiansted was introduced. Ron de Lugo had moved to St. Croix from St. Thomas and worked at Radio Station WIVI which was located at Fort Louise Augusta in Christiansted.

The 1958 - 1959 Festival was headed by Luz James and the co-chairman's chair was Ulric Benjamin. The theme that year was "See You at The Village."

*The Festival Village on the Christiansted Wharf.*
*Photo by Raymond Jacobs    St. Croix Festival Booklet    Fair Use*

The committee was late in getting organized for the 1959 – 1960 Festival, so it was decided that there would be no chairman or co-chairman but a steering committee instead. Jenny Thurland and Ruth Williams Klint held the key posts in Christiansted and Delta Dorsch in Frederiksted. That year the two committees made separate plans so that both towns could provide fun and cheer for its people during the Yuletide festivities.

Gerard Doward in *The Glory Days of Frederiksted* recalled the Festival Village in that town. "It was outside unlike the ones we have today where people sell from booths. Tables would be set up under a large gallery like what is today the Oscar Henry building. Then the village moved to the tennis court by Fort Frederick."

Mr. Doward described his family's involvement with Christmas Festivals Food Fairs over the years in Frederiksted:

> My mother, Mrs. Alma Doward, participated in just about every Festival Village until about the late 70s or early 80s. She would sell food, so my sisters and I would have to help prepare the meals. We worked very hard to make sure everything was done well. Mother would sell things like kallaloo, souse, potato salad, fry fish, and roast pork. A lot of time and effort was put into preparing those dishes because cooks were known for the good food they sold. Years later my sisters, Daphne and Anna, would sell food at the Food Fairs in Frederiksted by the Oscar Henry Building just as our mother did for the Old Time Festival.

*Mrs. Alma Doward with a tray on her head in a Festival Parade.*
*Photo by Fritz Henle     St. Croix Festival Booklet     Fair Use*

The Festival Booklet for December 28, 1962 to January 7, 1963, shows the continued growth of Festival on St. Croix. The booklet editor was Henville Rogiers and Sylvia Schjang was in charge of circulation. The Steering Committee members were Larry Motta as Chairman, Jenny Thurland Vice-Chairman and Ruth Williams Klint was Secretary-Treasurer. Sylvia Schjang had the Queen Contest committee, the Young Democrats handled the Festival Village, and the stage was built by Burnup and Sims. The other committees were Floats under the direction of Phyllis Saunders, Photographs by Egil Klint and Fritz Henle, the Farmer's Fair with Amy McKay and Rudy Henderson, Lights by Minnard Jones, David C. Canegata, Jr., and Arol Steele, Music by Darryl Walcott, Decorations by Jimmy Roebuck and Parades with Monroe Clendenen and David C. Canegata, Jr.

Some of the 1962-1963 booklet's sponsors were The Virgin Islands Title and Trust Company, Bruce and Mary Millar, Hamilton House Restaurant and Cocktail Bar, Harvey Alumina Virgin Islands, Inc., Virgin Islands Marine Industries, Inc., Cavanagh's Butik, Inc., Antilles Surveys, Inc., M. Hubert Hilder, The Pantry, El Capricho, Manocan's Auto Parts and Sales, and Camacho's Self Service.

The Festival Program had a wide variety of entertainment events and featured local bands. The Festival Village opened on Friday, December 28th with the Grand Queen Coronation ceremonies and music provided by the Vibratones Orchestra. Dr. Randall James played with this band.

On December 29th, Pedrito Altieri and his famous Grapetree Bay Steel Band played and there was a Limbo and Twist Contest for children and adults. Pedrito, who was originally from Puerto Rico, worked as an engineer at the Bethlehem Sugar Factory and started a steel band that played at the Grapetree Bay Hotel. Pedrito had a musical album and he even took local acts to Puerto Rico and New York City.

On the Sunday night December 30th, The St. Croix Community Band conducted by Mr. Peter G. Thurland, Sr., gave a musical concert. The next day there was the Agricultural Farmers Fair at the Public Market Place supervised by Rudy Henderson. There was a fireworks display on the Christiansted Wharf directed by H. L. Canegata.

*Adelaide "Cook Addie" George, the author's paternal great-grandmother, dancing to the beat of Pedrito Altieri's Steel Band. Pedrito is standing right behind "Cook Addie."*
*Photo by Will Thurland*        *Will Thurland Photo Collection*

New Year's Day of 1963 had two parades. The Children's Parade in Christiansted scheduled to start at 8:30 A.M. and was directed by Club 57. At 2:30 P.M., Frederiksted had a Grand New Year's Day Parade. At 8:30 P.M. that night there was a Native Calypso Singers Contest.

The Festival continued the next day January 2, 1963, with a concert by the Vibratones Orchestra under the leadership of Rudy Schulterbrandt. Mr. Schulterbrandt would years later be a Commissioner of Agriculture for the Virgin Islands Government. The following night the Gladiators Steel Band of Frederiksted under the leadership of Cephas Rodgers provided the musical entertainment.

The Christiansted High School Band conducted by Mr. Angelo Marasco gave a concert on January 4th in the Festival Village. Mr. Marasco took the C.H.S. Band to the New York's World Fair a few years later accompanied by Peter G. Thurland, Sr., and they were recognized on the popular Ed Sullivan television show.

The Bonny Steel Band led by Bernard Edney performed on the Christiansted stage on January 5, 1963. On January 6th the Christiansted High School Aquinaldo Singers led by Austin de Chabert performed Spanish songs. Mr. de Chabert taught Spanish at Christiansted High School and later at the College of the Virgin Islands, St. Croix campus, for several years.

The Grand Three King's Day Parade scheduled to begin at 3:00 P.M. was held in Christiansted on January 7, 1963, followed by a Steel Band Contest the same evening. The Festival Village closed at 11:59 P.M. sharp.

Aurelia Cepeda Estrill remembers her brother Floyd Henderson had convinced her to run in the Queen competition for the 1962-1963 Festival. She recalled, "At that time, the winner was the person who sold the most tickets. The tickets were white, had your name and number and stated what you were running for. I think it was five cents a ticket. Unfortunately, I did not sell the most tickets."

Reminiscing on the Parade Aurelia said, "Juan Luis, who later became the third elected governor of the Virgin Islands, was my chauffer and he had a red car. The dresses were long so the committee put us in a convertible. I remember that sometimes the Queen and her escorts dressed over at the Hotel on the Cay and they came over on a boat and went to the stage on the Wharf."

A few of the sponsors for the 1964-1965 Festival Booklet were Masonry Products, Inc., Island Dairies, V.I. Times, First Federal Savings Bank, Toby's Interiors, Inc., The New Saint Croix Savings Bank, Burnup and Sims, Inc., The Office Restaurant, Paint Locker, Café de Paris, Kissler's Gift Shop, Dolphin Restaurant and Bar, The Mahogany Inn, Magic Isle Beach Club, Unitime Corporation, V. I. Photo Supply, Suarez Supermarket, Alejo's, Richards & Ayer Associates, Independent Roofing & Sheet Metal Co., Mary O'Neill Gift Shop, and Rohlsen Sales, Co. Inc.

Ruth Moore wrote in the *Arts in the U.S. Virgin Islands* publication, "Mr. Clendenen led the Festival Parade on St. Croix in 1965. He no longer dressed as a pirate but in top hat and tails." Mrs. Leola Carroll, wife of legislator Eric Carroll, remembered Monroe dressed as Uncle Sam in the parades.

Over the years several festival troupes and their organizers were prominent in the parades. The Old Time Festival saw many changes throughout the years as it became the St. Croix Festival and the local government took charge of the Christmas festivities. The Boxing Day masquerades have disappeared from our Christmas culture of merrymaking and performing in the streets. The Festival Village in Christiansted had several different locations from the Wharf, Parade Ground, Watergut, Estate Slob and back to Parade Ground now known as the D.C. Canegata Ballpark. For several years the villages and parades alternated between both towns. A gubernatorial decision was made to have the Festival Parades in Frederiksted which resulted in the Festival Village and both the Children's and Adult's Parades being held in that town.

# FLOYD HENDERSON

## Festival Troupe Leader

Floyd Henderson, a Hillsider from Christiansted, organized his own Festival Parade troupes for 35 years and also participated in parades with the J & J Fun Troupe.

"The first year for me was in 1953, when we had a Limbo Troupe. We were young and the group carried a stick to dance around and under. I used to dance the Limbo that Mrs. Anna Brodhurst taught us. She had gone to Trinidad, saw it and came back and taught us how to dance it. I was in a youth club that had meetings at St. John's Anglican Church Hall. I decided to have the troupe and about 50 young people participated. We dressed up with a calypso shirt made out of a silky taffeta. It was a red shirt and we wore white pants. The female members wore a skirt with frills in the front and back. The troupe's name was "Floyd Henderson Coming Down the Road." I was about 13, maybe 15 years old. I believe we had to dance to another troupe's music with them in front and we were behind the band. It could have been Ralph "Rally" Phillipus' scratch band."

In a *St. Croix Avis* 2002 article for the 50th Anniversary of Festival, Floyd Henderson stated that he remembers the big yellow buses that would pick people up from neighborhoods and take them to the Festival. His limbo dance troupe was among the many who got on the bus. "The buses parked by the Alexander Theater in Sunday Market in Christiansted and would take people to Frederiksted. Mrs. Ann Abramson sent three buses and there was no charge. As a matter of fact, a bus came by my house in Estate Richmond to take my troupe to the parade.

After high school I was drafted into the United States Army and was sent to Germany. Over there I danced the Limbo. After the bivouac maneuvers, we were given a party and each section did something. My section was more into playing baseball. I had carried a calypso shirt and we made a Limbo stick with cotton on both ends. We lit a fire to the cotton and so we danced. The bigwigs, like the colonels, liked it and asked if we could do it at their officer's club.

In 1960, for a ceremony held in Washington, D.C. at the White House, three of us, who were youth delegates from the Virgin Islands, were honored. Maddie Pike from St. Thomas, a Sprauve from St. John and I from St. Croix. Maddie and another person sewed a shirt for me. Everybody there was into the music and seeing my dancing the Limbo with fire on the stick.

*Floyd Henderson dancing the Limbo at Grapetree Bay Hotel on St. Croix.*
*He also performed in Santurce, Puerto Rico along with Pedrito Altieri.*
*Courtesy of Floyd Henderson*

The Parades first started in Christiansted but I can't remember when they started in Frederiksted. I have had several children and adult troupes. My children's troupes used to be Indians and Zulus.

We had Norma Pemberton, Celeste Natta, and a gentleman from St. Lucia, Cuthbert Anthony who made the big costumes. I believe his wife also sewed. Inez and Maria Hall helped make head pieces and used to be at my house until late working on those pieces.

Some of the troupe members were Annette Hendricks, Daryl Roebuck, Mario Moorhead, Lloyd Bough, Edgar Iles, Edgar Ross, a Tutein, and Esta Danielson who was very graceful and carried the big costumes. Gordon Finch, David and Marion Motta had good parts in the Parades.

One year we had St. Croix Under Seven Flags and another troupe was Under the Sea with fishes. Luz James, Sr. was the commentator for The Kites Troupe. He stood on the wall by the Christiansted Post Office and announced our entry. The St. Croix Under Seven Flags entry was very good, and Governor Juan Luis was so pleased that he used to talk about it all the time. The shirts had a big American flag on one side and on the next side it had a British flag.

A big troupe The Casino Fantasy had waiter girls, and Ferris Wheels. I asked Merlina James, a teacher at the Christiansted High School, to have one of her class be the tourists in my troupe. There were headpieces with nickels, quarters, fifty cents and paper money. I remember that parade was in Frederiksted, and people came and pulled off the money.

The Flowers of the Island was a very beautiful troupe with white, red and lilac bougainvillea flowers. There was an advertisement with that troupe that ran on television for about six months.

One time we got five hundred bucks for the 50th Semi Centennial Parade and also got a trophy. We have won first and second prize many times. The first year we entered we didn't win because of big troupes like Miss Jenny Thurland and the Canegatas.

The Parade route started on the Christiansted Wharf, went down Company Street, passed the Alexander Theater and turned down on King Street. Other parades came down Company Street and by St. John's Anglican Church, and then turned down to Watergut when the Festival Village was kept there.

*Floyd Henderson leading his troupe by Bassin Triangle in Christiansted*
*for the St. Croix Festival's 35th Anniversary Parade.*
*Photo by Karen C. Thurland*

*Floyd Henderson in his kite costume in a Festival Parade.*
*Courtesy of Floyd Henderson*

Some other troupes were organized by Mrs. Anna Brodhurst, Mrs. Hilda England and Shirley "Lines" had majorettes. The Canegata troupe had Lito Valls, Carmen Canegata and Kay O' Reilly Motta. The Clowns were organized by Young and Isherwood whose office was next to Government House. Blanca Polanco used to be in that troupe. When they stopped doing Parades they gave me all their makeup for my troupe.

We started to prepare for the troupe from early July or August. By October it was more rapid preparation. I got broken cement bags from VI Cement and we fixed that paper over the wires before we put on the materials. For the Lantern Parades we used to dress in pajamas and danced in the streets.

The Festival Parades today are nice and beautiful. My sister's daughter Darisse Dowling have a troupe called Regal Dynasty that can have from 300 to over 500 members. The costumes are the latest thing like what you see in Trinidad and Rio, Brazil."

# MRS. LILLIAN BAILEY

## Culture Bearer and Festival Troupe Leader

Lillian Bailey was an original member of the St. Croix Women League and participated in the annual St. Croix Christmas Festival, organizing troupes for twelve consecutive years. In 1960, she founded the Festive Club of Frederiksted and won several awards for her parade entries. She also participated in the St. Thomas Carnival and held cultural productions on that island.

Mrs. Bailey founded the St. Croix Cultural Dancers, Inc. in 1970, and she worked toward the preservation of local dances and music. This organization was later led by Alphonsine Russell. The St. Croix Heritage Dancers is a spinoff from the St. Croix Cultural Dancers.

Anastasia "Anna" Doward remembers the troupes that Lillian Bailey sponsored during the early years of Festival. Anna knew Mrs. Bailey from St. Patrick's Church and had participated in a few parade entries with the troupe.

*Mrs. Lillian Bailey, a Frederiksted troupe leader.*
*Courtesy of Vertilee B. Daniel     The Glory Days of Frederiksted*

Mrs. Bailey had several troupes such as the Deck of Cards which she had entered twice in the parades. The second time was when Mrs. Bailey got sick. I was a member of that troupe and noticed that she seemed tired and was not feeling well. I think one year they did a David and Goliath troupe. An entry for the Emancipation parade featured someone in a Statute of Liberty costume.

Vertilee Bailey Daniel, her daughter, participated in the parades with her mother. Other troupe participants included people from St. Patrick's Church and the Frederiksted community such as Gwendolyn Lucas and Dolores Abramson Iles.

*The Garden of the West Indies Troupe performing in Frederiksted. Iris
Bailey is one of the troupe members.*
*Photo by Axel Ovesen*             *St. Croix Landmarks Society*

*The Garden of the West Indies Troupe going down Fisher Street in Frederiksted.*
*Photo by Axel Ovesen                                St. Croix Landmarks Society*

In the early 1960s, Odelia Nesbitt who worked at Merwin was one of the seamstresses. Heado and Anthony, who were from Trinidad, helped make the costumes and the head pieces.

Vertilee Bailey Daniel in *The Glory Days of* Frederiksted wrote about an honor her mother received. "In 1970, Mrs. Bailey was the recipient of Merit from the Festival Club of Frederiksted for her "selfless and devoted efforts and service in the founding, organization and development of cultural and festival activities in the U. S. Virgin Islands."

# MRS. ANNA WHITEHEAD BRODHURST

## Old Time Christmas Festival Organizer and Troupe Leader

Mrs. Anna Brodhurst was a member of the Women's League that started the annual Old Time Christmas Festival on St. Croix in December 1952, and she had troupes and later appeared as an individual entry in many parades.

Sandra Brodhurst Fields, one of her granddaughters, remembers that there were several troupes and she participated in one of the entries. "I remember my grandmother going down the street dancing wearing a wide skirt and holding an umbrella. We danced in and out in a circle."

Canute Brodhurst, her grandson, recalls when the Festival Parades started by the Golden Cow in Bassin Triangle. "My parents were in a troupe depicting the Romans. People used to call my grandmother "The Christmas Tree" because she wore everything green and also had a green and red parasol."

*Mrs. Anna Brodhurst with her granddaughter Sandra parading in Sunday Market in Christiansted.*

*Courtesy of Sandra Brodhurst Fields*

*A Food Fair in the Christiansted Vegetable Market.*
*Photo by Egil Klint      St. Croix Festival Booklet      Fair Use*

In 1956, the St. Croix Hotel Association acknowledged the community service provided by Mrs. Brodhurst to the annual Christmas Festival celebrations. In a letter to the Festival Committee the association wrote about her contributions and its impact:

> The St. Croix Hotel Association wishes to take this opportunity to recognize the splendid unselfish service that Mrs. Anna Brodhurst has rendered, through the years, to the island of St. Croix in her devoted work of organizing and directing the planning of the Christmas Festival Committee.

The Hotel Association further noted a significant contribution Mrs. Brodhurst made to the Christmas Festival:

> It was through her efforts and personal support that Steel Bands were first introduced to our Island. This has resulted in creating such interest in this unique type of music, which is a product of the West Indies, that now St. Croix proudly enjoys several Steel Bands that have been organized. The impact as an attraction to visitors to our island is tremendous and our reputation for affording this attraction is constantly growing in the States.

The Association concluded by stating that this one achievement is not the only contribution that Mrs. Brodhurst has made:

> We cite this one instance of which there are many, to show the benefits that we all enjoy as a direct result of the untiring efforts of Mrs. Brodhurst in the successful promotion of our Christmas Festival.

The Festival Committee for the 50th Golden Anniversary of the St. Croix Festival hung a photograph of Mrs. Anna Brodhurst in the Christiansted Market honoring her as the head of the Women's League, the Festival's first organizers.

# AMELIA "AMY" PETERSEN JOSEPH

## Eve's Garden Festival Troupe Leader

Amelia "Amy" Petersen Joseph organized Festival troupes for fifteen years keeping up the tradition started by her mother, Mrs. Evadney Neazer Petersen, who worked with the Festival committee and had troupes for twenty-five or twenty-six years. Amelia better known as "Amy" to her many friends got involved from young with the Eve's Garden troupe along with her mother from the first year of Festival. She has also worked with several Festival Committees and committees at her school, the Claude O' Markoe Elementary School.

Amy remembers masqueraders when she was young. She recollected, "You heard them coming. We lived at Harden Gut and the masqueraders came through there from Estate Concordia. We used to hide under the bed because the masqueraders controlled your behavior. Sometimes I would peep through the windows upstairs and I saw one or two mocko jumbies. This was in the late 1940s and early 50s in Frederiksted.

Masqueraders dressed in old clothes like a crocus bag with scrap material on a skirt. Some would have dry grass and layers of cloth. All parts of their bodies were covered so I didn't know men from women. They had a veil over their face or a wire mask. Some might have on an old hat decorated with flowers. They did performances in the streets. Some depicted a story from long ago. A few masqueraders came down the street and threw flour on you and ran off. I saw a Bull with the horns in a full costume with a white flour bag underneath and thread and grass through it. The bull horns were glued to the mask or headpiece.

The drums, the bass and kettle drums, and the steel squash were the main instruments. When children and some adults heard the music, they scattered. The masqueraders had a whip that they would hit on the street. Some masqueraders had tall hats with feathers, and some had cloth masks, a tight cloth stocking. You are not to see the masquerader's face.

My mother Evadney Neazer Petersen was a public health nurse who for many years took care of people in Frederiksted town and throughout the countryside. She was also a midwife who delivered babies at all hours. Additionally, she conducted clinics for expectant mothers and visited patients who could not visit the clinic. "Madame Pete," as she was called, also gave injections as part of the immunization effort.

*Mrs. Evadney Neazer Petersen was the organizer of the Eve's Garden*
*Festival troupes and a member of several festival committees.*
*Courtesy of Arlene Petersen Abraham*

Amy Petersen Joseph described her mother's participation with the Christmas Festival in *The Glory Days of Frederiksted.* "From the onset Madame Pete became involved in the planning of the revival of Festival. She became an active member of the Committee in 1952 and organized entries which participated in Frederiksted, Christiansted, as well as the St. Thomas Carnival on several occasions.

The Eve's Garden troupes I remember are the Sun, Moon and Stars and David and Goliath which we performed in front of the judges. We had Paradise Lost, Paradise Regained and the Bull Fighters. She was a public health nurse for many years who walked throughout the town and the country estates carrying a medical bag and later developed a hip problem.

One year we had a Sailboat Regatta troupe. We had big size fans for our Chinese Dynasty troupe. The Hawaiian troupe had a roast pig on a stick, hula hoops and beach stuff like fishing nets and swimsuits. Another year we had a Chain Gang troupe with black and white stripped costumes. Members had a ball on their foot, and we even had correction officers pretending like they were beating the prisoners.

There was a Candy Cane troupe for which we ordered red and white pajamas for the costumes. Then, we had a Natural Rain Forest troupe with a fountain. There were flamboyant and hibiscus trees for that troupe. We didn't get first prize that year. One year we had a windmill on a float and another year a troupe with bonnets and wire skirts. Troupes with cultural themes included the Market Women, the Mexicans, and the Mardi Gras.

I had a children's troupe called the Lilliputians with a big man on casters with wheels to pull. We had different fishes one year. Then I had The Lady Who Lived in the Shoe with a grandmother and her children. Another year I had children plaiting the Maypole with ribbons and they did the braiding and the unbraiding.

Maria "Joy" Thomas Lewis, Cheryl Soto and I started the Sun Setters Majorettes. We met at the Arthur A. Richards Jr. High School and did that for three to four years before other schools came out with majorette troupes.

Our last troupe was a cultural troupe called Old Time Masqueraders with Quadrille dancers who had head pieces made with madras cloth. The female Quadrille dancers had a white peasant blouse and a wide Quadrille skirt with a wire frame and can can skirts that were multilayered and full of frills and ruffles. There was a big mocko jumbie character on the float. I always had a floupe, which is a combined troupe and float.

*Mrs. Amelia "Amy" Petersen Joseph has carried on the family tradition of organizing Eve's Garden Festival Troupes.*
*Courtesy of Amy Petersen Joseph*

I stopped organizing troupes for several reasons. I paid Express Band $1,000.00 for playing music on Parade Day and had to get a big truck for the band. Then, I had to pay the driver his salary for the day. The band needed a generator and gas. Insurance was also an issue. I had to build the troupe and make costumes. It was ridiculously expensive even though we had sponsors.

The fabrics for the costumes came from New York so that was an off-island trip. The costumes had to be sewn and the head pieces decorated. Some people would say they are coming for the costume the night before the parade and don't show up with the money or pick up the costume.

The Festival parades today, I am disappointed with because there are more of a bacchanal than a festival. The way participants dress, they are not depicting anything. You are seeing almost naked bodies with feathers and wire. Years ago, each troupe had a theme and was organized around that theme. Today people dancing and gyrating on the ground. It is an embarrassment to me. We adapt other people's culture and ignore our own, even the children's troupes."

*Eve's Garden Donkey Troupe.*
*Courtesy of Amy Petersen Joseph*

*A mocko jumbie doll dressed in madras made by Amy Joseph. She makes handcrafted cultural dolls in different size for tables, floor models and ornaments for the Christmas holidays*
*Courtesy of Amy Petersen Joseph*

# THE GENTLEMEN OF JONES

According to Melba Canegata Biggs, The Gentlemen of Jones has been involved in Festival from the very first year. "Minnard "Jonesy" Jones had a bar downstairs where Cedie and Lois Canegata lived on Strand Street in Christiansted. The guys used to hang out there and decided to enter the parade wearing top hats. It was a lot of fun and people were looking for things to do."

Ulric E. Benjamin, Sr., and David C. Canegata, Jr., in a February 1997 *Pride Magazine* article on The Gentleman of Jones related how the troupe got organized. "The group loved baseball and each Sunday after church they met at Parade Ground, today the David C. Canegata Ball Park outside Christiansted. This sports group gathered at Jones' establishment and planned to enter the Old Time Festival Parade."

The article continued. "It was Arol Steele and the Canegata brothers, Cedie and Lloyd, who got their fellow members to form a troupe for the Parade. They agreed on a costume of top hat and tails, together with walking sticks and one member in a handmade, police-type outfit. The men paraded down the streets and following behind them was Lloyd Canegata's jeep "Melinda" loaded with refreshments and driven by Cedric Canegata."

The story further notes that the group did not have a name when they were scheduled to go on the stage but Rexford Hodge, father of Lt. Governor Derek and Attorney Winston Hodge, told the parade officials the name of the group was "Gentlemen of Jones," and that name has been carried on throughout the years.

David C. Canegata Jr., Rexford Hodge, James C. Canegata, Keith Forbes, Oswald O. Schjang, Randall N. James, Minnard Jones, Arrol Steele

THE GENTLEMEN OF JONES - THREE KINGS DAY PARADE 1953

*The Gentlemen of Jones dressed in top hats and coats for the 1953 Festival Parade.*
*Courtesy of the Gentlemen of Jones*

Benjamin and Canegata described the lighting of the town of Christiansted as one of the group's contributions to the St. Croix community. "The Gentlemen strung incandescent white lights across the streets with the bulbs and wire being donated by businesses and individuals in the community. All of Company and King Streets were aglow with lights, with crowds of people strolling happily through town to enjoy the display. Governor Morris F. de Castro was so impressed that he invited the Gentlemen of Jones to a reception at Government House and wrote them a letter of commendation."

*The Gentlemen of Jones decked out in their top hats and coats for their 50th Anniversary Parade. Front row: Left to right, Louis Hassell, Jr., Dave Davis, and Norbin Felix. Second row: Left to right, Senator Kenneth Gittens, Freddie Pimentel, Jr., Ralph Munchez, Jr., Edwin Rosario, Roy Rodgers, Gerald Evans and Conrad Knowles. Third row: Left to right, Peter Bandoo, Conrad Hoover and Marc Biggs. On the float: Left to right, Lambert Demester, Darius George, Craig Williams, Jr., Robbie Ramsingh and Mitch Mitchell. Robert "Bob" Moorehead, historian for the Gentlemen of Jones, identified the members in the photo and also shared information about the group.*
*Courtesy of the Gentlemen*

The Gentlemen of Jones have continued to light the streets of Christiansted ever since 1952, the first year of the St. Croix Festival, and the year 2022 will be 70 years of active participation in the Christmas Festival. They have had such troupes as The Roaring Twenties, Super Heroes, and numerous others.

Donna Christian Christensen, former Delegate to Congress, recalls her father Judge Almeric Christian being a member of The Gentlemen of Jones and also Dr. Randall James, Herbert "Stubby" Grigg and Clinton Lang. Some of the other members were Keith Forbes, the Canegatas, the Schjangs and the Langs.

Ole Christensen has been a member of the group since 1956 and stated, "Jonesy" was the electrical teacher at the Christiansted High School and got his students, like myself and "Stubby" Grigg involved in putting up lights in Christiansted. Ole stated, "It was Arol Steel and Keith Forbes who decided that lights should be put up in town. Arol Steel went around collecting funds from the businesses in town. The lights the class put up were big bulbs."

Clinton Lang was in high school when he got involved with The Gentlemen of Jones and was a member for many years. He stated, "Jonesy was my Electrical class instructor. I attended St. Mary's School in the mornings and public school in the afternoons for their vocational program. I used to put together the string of lights for the streets and repair the strings or replace bulbs before the following year's activities. Besides Jones being my teacher I sold gas at Christiansted Utilities and Jonesy's Bar was next door and I carried over ice to his establishment. I stopped in after work and eventually became a member of the group."

Mr. Lang further explained his role in the troupe. "I was the electrical person but never went up the ladder and I used to cook for the troupe. I had an oven so I did biscuits and lechon."

According to Melba Canegata Biggs it was Lois Canegata who started the women's section of the troupe. "The troupes were The Mexicans, The Jingle Bells, The Red and White and one year we were Pirates. Lois Canegata, Maria Schjang and Sylvia Schjang did most of the sewing of the costumes. Some of the members of the women section of the troupe were Leona Woodson, Virginia Christian, Carmen Canegata, Eva Forbes, and Aracelis Bermudez."

*Men in top hats riding in a convertible in a Christiansted Festival Parade.*
*St. Croix Christmas Festival Booklet*　　　　　　　　　　　　　*Fair Use*

Lois Messer Canegata reminisced about the first time the women came out for the Festival Parade. "The first Festival Troupe we had was Martha Washington. Maria Schjang and I were the organizers of that troupe. Members of the troupe bought their own materials and made costumes. We hired a band to play for us and we had music provided by the Watergonians Steel Band for several years. My house had silver dust and sequins in the wooden floor up to a year later. As to the future of Festival, it needs more organization and must get back to cultural things."

Claire Canegata Motta remembered the troupes for the Gentlemen of Jones. "We had Martha Washington, Indians, Egyptians, Mexicans and we had women in troupes up to 1964 or 1965. We enjoyed the parades when we first started but then it got a little too wild."

Ulric Benjamin, Sr., remarked that in 1991, the St. Croix Chamber of Commerce presented a beautiful plaque to the Gentlemen, recognizing and complementing them on their civic services and he, as Chairman, accepted on behalf of the group.

# GENEVIEVE "JENNY" THURLAND

# Festival Troupe Leader

Genevieve "Jenny" Thurland was an active member of the Festival Committee and an organizer of several troupes. She was a musician probably taught by her father Peter G. Thurland, Sr. who founded the St. Croix Community Band. Miss Jenny played the organ in various churches when she was a teenager and played at St. Anne's Catholic Church at Barrenspot free of charge for many years.

Miss Jenny back in 1982 in preparation for an article for the Festival booklet which commemorated the thirtieth anniversary of Festival recalled her experiences. She told me about Mrs. Hilda England and Mrs. Anna Brodhurst and their efforts to organize the Old Time Festival. She told me about masquerades, the Blue Bells, the La France Dancers and Mother Hubbard groups of long ago. She also spoke about Magnus, Viggo Roberts and Monroe Clendenen. Jenny Thurland's first troupe was The Gypsy Fortune Teller and she sat in a donkey cart with a green crystal ball in her hand. I remember seeing that green ball in her living room for many years.

I am elated that I have copies of the pictures she shared with me because her photos, trophies and other Festival memorabilia like the green crystal ball and winning trophy were damaged when she lost her roof in 1989 to Hurricane Hugo.

*Genevieve "Jenny" Thurland sitting in a donkey cart with a crystal ball for her Gypsy Fortune Teller Troupe. This was her first entry in the Old Time Christmas Festival Parades.*
*Courtesy of Genevieve "Jenny" Thurland*

She is best remembered by family and friends for her Chinese Troupe. The troupe members dressed in Oriental costumes and carried baskets while others twirled parasols as they danced in the streets.

One year the troupe's theme was the Mikado of Japan, which was based on the operetta by Gilbert and Sullivan. Her brother Will Thurland built a rickshaw cart for that troupe.

Norma Dennis Mason reminisced about festival parades of bygone days. "When I think of the St. Croix Festival I think of Jenny Thurland and Hilda England. Every year Miss Jenny had a troupe. I have been in Jenny Thurland's troupes several times and she helped me organize the Bumble Bees children's troupe. Mrs. Hilda England started the Children's Parade because of the schools and getting the children involved in Festival.

*Genevieve "Jenny" Thurland with a cart for her Festival Troupe in*
*Sunday Market in Christiansted.*
*Photo by Will Thurland*          *Will Thurland Photo Collection*

Back in the 50s, Miss Jenny had a beautiful Chinese troupe and I was a teenager about 12 or 13 years old. My mother took my sister Lorelei and myself home after the Parade. I remember there was food for the troupe members from St. Thomas at the Thurland's house on Hospital Street. The following year I did a children's version of that troupe.

One year Miss Jenny was a Bull portraying the old-time masquerades. I loved to see her dance and she had a style to kill you. She could' ah dance and she used to enjoy herself. I remember practicing the dance steps on the basketball court by the Fort in Christiansted where the Festival Village would later be built."

*Genevieve "Jenny" Thurland in a Chinese costume for Festival Parade.*
*Courtesy of Michelle Thurland-Martinez*

Doreen Rissing Hay participated in several troupes because she and Jenny Thurland were cousins. So naturally, family members joined in the troupes. She laughingly said, "I used to go to her house and helped prepare food for the people from St. Thomas who were in her troupe. We made chicken, roast pork, goat, rice and stuffing. For desserts we did cakes and pies. The drinks were local favorites such as maubi, soursop drink, and tamarind. Jenny used to make a nice maubi. The troupe members went up to her house to eat after the parade.

Now during the parades, they carried water or stopped by the festival booth to get something to drink especially when that hot sun hit them. And considering that we had some elder members in the troupe and we had to line up early for the parade.

I remember the Matadors and the Japanese Troupes and liked the costumes she wore in the parades. Jenny was the Bull and I believe we won second prize for that troupe. We performed on the Christiansted Wharf and had a good time."

*Genevieve "Jenny" Thurland dancing with her Chinese troupe in a Festival Parade.*
*Photo by Axel Ovesen*                     *St. Croix Landmarks Society*

*Genevieve "Jenny" Thurland portraying a Bull in a Festival Parade in Christiansted.*
*Photo from Will Thurland Film Collection*

Doreen summarized her experiences with Festival activities saying, "I have been in almost anything with music. I never miss anything and I was a dancer. I plait the Maypole on the Wharf and was in Lantern Parades. Those Lantern Parades used to be real nice. We dressed up in a costume that we used before and made our own lanterns. We made lanterns with paper and put candles inside. Some had sticks for you to hold the lanterns."

Dr. Eleanor Thraen of St. Thomas was a member of several of Jenny Thurland's troupes. "I got to know about the troupe because of my family's close relationship with the Maduros from Savan. Elma Maduro was my godmother, and her family were good friends with Jenny Thurland. I stayed at Jenny's house because I was a teenager and that was the only place my mother would let me stay away from home. Jenny was a fun-loving person who was down to earth. She called a spade a spade.

Mrs. Alice Brady Amaro and Mrs. Bianca LaBorde were very close friends from St. Thomas and both worked in the Cooperative Store on the waterfront. They came to St. Croix for the parades."

*The Bull and Matadors performing on stage at the Christiansted Wharf.*
*Photo from Will Thurland Film Collection*

*The Thurland House at No. 1 Hospital Street in Christiansted in the
1950s where family and friends viewed the Festival Parade going up
to Parade Ground. Many friends from St. Thomas, St. John and the
U.S. mainland stopped by during the festive season and especially
on parade days.*
*Photo by Will Thurland*　　　　　*Will Thurland Photo Collection*

*The Thurland House on Hospital Street with family and friends on the porch. Derek Parilla, a mocko jumbie from St. Thomas, a member of Alli Paul's Original Mocko Jumbie troupe, left the parade and stopped by and asked "Miss Jenny" for a drink of water.*
*Photo by Karen C. Thurland*

St. Croix Festival Troupes also went over to St. Thomas for their Carnival. A notice in the *Daily News* of March 29, 1957, titled "Carnival Groups Plan Surprises" wrote about planned Crucian participation in that year's parade. "Troupes from St. Croix: Petersen's St. Croix Pirates, Genevieve Thurland's troupe, and Mrs. Martin's group of twenty majorettes." St. Thomas troupes also came over to participate in the St. Croix Festival Parades.

Jenny Thurland participated in several Festival parades and worked on several St. Croix Festival committees. She later got involved in local politics and in the 1960s served as the Democratic National Committeewoman of the Virgin Islands for several years.

# LILLIANA BELARDO DE O'NEAL

## Senator and Community Activist

L illiana Belardo de O'Neal grew up in the Estate La Grande Princesse Village outside of the town of Christiansted. She has been involved in Christmas Festival activities for many years and has valuable insight and information about the Puerto Rican involvement throughout the years.

Mrs. Belardo de O'Neal stated, "I got involved with Festival when I was in high school and helped my older sister who was a food vendor at the Christiansted waterfront and also with a high school presentation. Professor Austin de Chabert had a group of us going around singing Aguinaldos, Christmas Spanish songs. After high school I was in several troupes for the parades. I organized the King Midas Troupe, everything he touched turned to gold, and won Second Prize.

It was the Frederiksted group that really organized the Three Kings Day celebration and that was done in the evening because we could not do it during the day. Chico Morales and Patrick Rucci Delgado started it. Miquel Duschesne brought the first Puerto Rican Queens to St. Croix. Fran Diaz, Felipe Cuencas along with Brigidio Martinez, a contractor, built the parade floats.

It was religious. The parade started with a star and then men dressed in costumes representing the Three Kings gave out candy and there would be a float with the Virgin Mary. After that we had groups that portrayed religious figures. It became the Three Kings Day Parade and alternated between Christiansted and Frederiksted.

*Men dressed as the Three Kings in a Crucian Rican Tramp in Christiansted.*
*Photo by Karen C. Thurland*

When the Festival Committee came in, they incorporated all the troupes and took over the real meaning of Three Kings Day. You see, Puerto Ricans celebrate Three Kings Day instead of Christmas. The Three King's gave gifts like candy and balloons when I was a young girl. When the committee moved the Adult Parade dates the significance of Three King's Day was lost.

One year I did Cleopatra going down the Nile on a barge and won second prize. The parades became too much showing of flesh and whining up so I stopped organizing troupes.

When I became a Senator I challenged them and had Three Kings Day parades on the sixth of January. We then had a third parade that I organized and had it in both towns. After I got out, Eddie Ortiz had it for a few years and he formed a non-profit organization. Now it is run by Emilito Torres and they gave gifts to kids in Estate Profit, Clifton Hill and Harvey Project on Three Kings Day keeping the tradition alive.

*Former Senator Lilliana Belardo de O'Neal served as the Republican National Committee Woman for several years and is a member of the Board of Elections for the St. Croix District.*
*Courtesy of Lilliana Belardo de O"Neal*

Every year that I was a Senator I had a boat ride to Vieques for their Carnival and we were invited to go to Fajardo and Luquillo. I carried the Sun Dancers Troupe and the steel band from the church. One year in Fajardo we had a big Indian troupe and the girls there were pulling feathers and other things off the men's costumes. The men were almost naked by the end of the parade!"

Lilliana and her husband Humberto were honored by the Crucian Christmas Festival at the Food, Arts and Crafts Fair in January 2018, for their years of participating in the Festival's Food Fair, Festival Villages and the Agricultural Fairs.

# MEMORIES OF PARADE TROUPES

The following are a few excerpts from conversations about the St. Croix Festival. So many stories are still left to be told and documented for future generations.

Ferne Joseph McAlpin, the 1968 – 1969 Festival Queen, described her mother Helen Joseph and her parade entries:

> I like when we were Marie Antoinette. My mother brought the costumes from New Orleans and we played real Mardi Gras. The guys were dressed in pants to their knees, had on white socks and wore admiral's hats. The women had wigs with curls. Claudette Forbes was the Queen for that parade. That troupe was fabulous.
>
> The music, in the beginning, was provided by the Vibratones but ninety per cent of the time the Ten Sleepless Knights played for our troupe. When we went to Frederiksted it was Milton Gordon who played for us. Helen Joseph was a musician and she had to have "live" music.

Ingrid Hendricks Bermudez of Christiansted fondly recalls being in a festival troupe in Christiansted as a young girl:

> When I was in second grade Mrs. Asta Kylvert James had a Pajama troupe and we won first prize that year. I went to her home across from Sylvia's Store on Company Street to try on my Chinese costume and the pointed hat that came

from New York. Years later, I participated in Festival by doing the makeup for the members of the Potpourri Troupe.

Other troupes I remember were Canegata with red and white candy strips. Hildred Edwards, Harry Edwards' daughter, danced at Parade Ground and Leona Barnes, who taught tap dance, and her dancers performed on the stage.

*Helen Joseph's Donkey Troupe in a Festival Parade in Christiansted. Her daughter Ferne Joseph McAlpin is in the middle of the group in the blue donkey costume.*
*Photo by Karen C. Thurland*

Meredith Clarke and several white continentals had the Clowns with red noses and they would ride on bikes and blow horns. Ms. Lois and Shirley had majorettes. Mrs. Hilda England's sister, who lived in Estate Contentment, had a troupe.

*A children's Clown Troupe on stage performing after a Festival Parade. Gotfred "Freddy" Thurland and George Thurland, the author's brothers, are at the left of the photo.*
*Photo by Will Thurland*                                        *Will Thurland Photo Collection*

*The St. Croix Community Band and a Majorette Troupe in a Festival Parade. Peter G. Thurland Sr., the Band Leader, is at the right with his Baritone instrument.*
*Photo by C. de Witt Rogers        St. Croix Festival Booklet            Fair Use*

*A Pirate troupe in Christiansted Near the Old Public Library. Protestant Cay and a bus is in the background.*
*Photo by Axel Ovesen*                                *St. Croix Landmarks Society*

Mrs. Eulalie Rivera of the Frederiksted Women's League recalled that Eulalie Jackson, Julio Delgado and Agnes Davila were among the members who worked with her. "We made the decorations and it was Julio Delgado who strung lights across the street. The Christmas Festival Parade was held on Christmas Second Day. The Three King's Parade came about because of the Puerto Ricans who lived on St. Croix. Today, we no longer see the Donkey, David and Goliath, and the Devil with horns. Our parades should reflect more of our culture. What we see now is more like Trinidad's Carnival."

Wayne James, former Virgin Islands Senator and historian, wrote in the *St Croix Avis* on December, 17, 2002, about the continued development of the Christmas Festival:

> By the 1970s, with the large influx of Trinidadians who had emigrated to the Virgin Islands beginning in the 1960s to work at Hess Oil, VI Carnival underwent a major transformation: troupes became less character-based and more theme-oriented, and less theatrical and more free-dance.
>
> Troupes became significantly larger – some containing upwards of 300 people – with features such as "King and Queen of the Band," those so designated supporting gigantic costumes; color-coordinated sections, each with a leader; beautiful abbreviated costumes, usually with leotard undergarments, collar-pieces and pieces covered with glittery fabrics and punctuated with ostrich plumes, and the ubiquitous flag-sticks, which could be seen waving in the air for almost as far as the eye could see.

Indeed, the influence of Trinidad Carnivals have been experienced throughout the entire Virgin Islands and continues to be the trend for troupe leaders and parade masqueraders. The African spirituality can still be witnessed in the Guardians of Our Culture Moko Jumbies led by Willard John, the West End Masqueraders and the AyAy Masqueraders. Our Christmas Festival will continue to evolve as it has grown into a major celebration and a tourist attraction as many people come out to have a good time.

Culture is dynamic not stagnant and changes come from within and outside. The Old Time Festival has grown to be called the St. Croix Festival and currently the Crucian Christmas Festival. The Festivals will be better than ever as we celebrate after the recent hurricane destruction and worldwide pandemic. The people need a release from emotional and financial stress and most certainly will enjoy the excitement of the pageantry and beauty of the Festival activities from the Queen and Prince and Princess contests, the Food Fairs, the Calypso Monarch competitions, the Jouvert early morning tramps, the Festival Village and of course, the Children's and Adult's Parades. The Festival will continue to evolve as additional activities are organized to enhance this annual Christmas celebration.

*A Festival Queen sitting in a convertible and the Rosedale Guest House and Shop on Hospital Street in Christiansted.*
*Photo by Will Thurland*                    *Will Thurland photo Collection*

*Festival Queen contestants dressed in their evening dresses walking in a Festival Parade on Fisher Street in Frederiksted.*
*Photo by Axel Ovesen*                                    *St. Croix Landmarks Society*

*A couple dancing in front of a Steel Band in a Festival Parade on Fisher Street in Frederiksted.*
*Photo by Axel Ovesen*                                    *St. Croix Landmarks Society*

*A masquerader with long peacock feathers entertaining a crowd in Christiansted, St. Croix.*
*Photo by Muriel Doolan*                    *Courtesy of Nancy Doolan*

# GLOSSARY

| | |
|---|---|
| Boxing Day | Christmas Second Day. |
| Burlap | Raw sugar was shipped in these sacks. |
| Calypso | Songs, usually improvised. Originally from Trinidad, they are characterized by humorous, political or sexual themes. |
| Crocus bag | Burlap sack. |
| Easter Monday | The Monday following Easter. Traditionally an island holiday. |
| Floupe | A parade entry at Festival time, consisting of a combined float and troupe. |
| Fraico | Shaved ice refreshment over which is poured different kinds of sweet flavored syrups. |
| Free Gut | The free colored quarters in Christiansted which was the only area in which free persons of color were allowed to live. |
| Gallows Bay | A neighborhood of Christiansted. |
| Hillsiders | Residents of the hillside areas of Christiansted, St. Croix. |
| Homestead | Land on which the head of household could farm and build a house. This program was started on St. Croix in 1934 when the federal government bought several estates and distributed small plots of land for farming. |
| Jump up | A dance. Usually said of a street dance, tramp or other disorganized dancing. |
| Kill Ting Pappy | Have a good time. |

| | |
|---|---|
| Limbo | A dance. Movements, with bodies thrown back, under a stick which is lowered after every passage, as far down as possible. |
| Masquerade | A social gathering of persons wearing masks and often costumes. |
| Masquerade Band | A musical ensemble in the past which attended masquerade troupes and consisted of one or more drums, a flute, triangle or steel, and a tail pipe. |
| Mocko Jumbie | A male stilt masquerader traditionally dressed in female attire. One of the most celebrated moko jumbies was "Magnus" (John Magnus Farrell) of St. Croix, who first appeared in in 1929. Recently the spelling has been changed to Moko instead of Mocko. |
| Pitchy Patchy | Ragged clothes. |
| Quadrille | A square dance of French origin. The national dance of the Virgin Islands of the United States. |
| Quelbe | The official music of the Virgin Islands of the United States. |
| Road March | A musical selection played most often at Festival or Carnival parades by steel bands and other musical groups. It originated in Trinidad. |
| Scratch band | A local musical ensemble consisting of flute, squash, bongos, triangle, tambourine, maracas (shek shek) and an ass pipe. |
| Steel Band | A musical group composed of people playing "steel pans." A pan being made from the ends of fifty-five-gallon oil drums cut off in different sizes. Discs are hammered, punched and tempered until grooved sections emit distinct pitches when tapped by rubber drumsticks. Other instruments used in a steel band are drums, drum trap sets, congas, tambourines and triangles. Steel pan music originated in Trinidad. |
| Tramp | Impromptu street dance done by revelers following a steel band or other musical group done during carnival or other festival time. |
| Troupe | A carnival or festival unit composed of individuals dressed in concert representing a group or depicting a story. |
| Watergut | A neighborhood of Christiansted, St. Croix. |
| Whit Monday | The day after Pentecost Sunday. |

# REFERENCES

Belardo de O'Neal, Lilliana. Christiansted, St. Croix. Interview, 22 February, 2022.

Canegata, Lois Messer. Christiansted, St. Croix. Interview, 21 December, 1992.

Browne, Iris. Christiansted, St. Croix. Interview, October – November, 2020.

Christian, Bradley & Gordon Henry, Yvonne. *Quadrille: The Official Dance of the U.S. Virgin Islands.*

Clendenen, Monroe Jr. Christiansted, St. Croix. Interview, 11 June, 2021.

Copemann, Dimitri. Christiansted, St. Croix. Interview, 7 June, 2021.

Doward, Anastasia. Frederiksted, St. Croix. Interview, 16 June, 2021.

Doward, Gerard. Frederiksted, St. Croix. Interview, 14 December, 2021.

Galloway, Ernest "Prince." Christiansted, St. Croix. Interview, February, 2021.

Harty, Cheyenne. "Crucian Christmas Festival Celebrates 50 Glorious Years." *The St. Croix Avis,* 15-16 December, 2002.

Hay, Doreen Rissing. Christiansted, St. Croix. Interview, 25 February, 2022.

Henderson, Floyd. Christiansted, St. Croix. Interview, March – April, 2021.

Heyliger, Cherra. "Christmas Spirit." *The St. Croix Avis*, 28-29 Dec. 2003.

Heyliger, Cherra. "Crucian Myths and Customs Were Sporting Fun." *The St. Croix Avis*, 30 Dec. 1989.

Heyliger, Cherra. "Origins of Our Festival." *The St. Croix Avis*, 8-9, January, 2006.

Heyliger, Cherra. "Xmas on St. Croix." *The St. Croix Avis*, 23 December, 1986.

Huntt, Yvonne. Christiansted, St. Croix. Interview, 26 February & 29 June, 2021.

Jacobs, Stanley. Christiansted, St. Croix. Interview, 29 April & 5 May, 2021.

James, Randall. New York City, New York. Interview, 16 July 2021 & 25 June 2022.

James, Wayne. *The St. Croix Avis*, 17 December 2002.

Joseph, Amelia "Amy" Petersen. Frederiksted, St. Croix, Interview, 6 & 11 May, 2021.

Knight, Mildred Rissing. Christiansted, St. Croix. Interview, 24 February, 2022.

Lang, Inez. Christiansted, St. Croix. Interview, 1 April, 2021.

Mason, Norma Dennis. Christiansted, St. Croix. Interview, 17 & 19, December 2020 & 12 January 2021.

Motta, Claire Canegata. Christiansted, St. Croix. Interview, 21 December, 1992.

McGregory, Jerrilyn. *One Grand Noise*: *Boxing Day in the Anglicized Caribbean World*. Jackson, Mississippi: University Press of Mississippi, 2021.

Nicholls, Robert W. *Old Time Masquerading in the U.S. Virgin Islands.* St. Thomas, U.S. Virgin Islands: The Virgin Islands Humanities Council, 1998.

Our Town Frederiksted. *The Glory Days of Frederiksted.* United States of America: 2004.

Pearson, Diana. "Kill 'Thing Pappy' On St. Croix." *The Daily News, 50th Anniversary Edition*, 1 Aug. 1980.

Richardson, Evelyn. *Seven Streets by Seven Streets.* NY: Edward W. Blyden Press, 1984.

Rivera, Eulalie C. *Growing Up On St. Croix: Recollections of a Crucian Girlhood.* St. Croix, VI: Antilles Graphics, revised 1984.

Rivera, Eulalie. Frederiksted, St. Croix. Interview, 18 December, 1992.

Schrader, Richard, Sr. Colquhoun, St. Croix. Interview, 28 May, 2021.

Schrader, Richard, Sr. *Maufe Quelbe and T'ing.* St. Croix: Antilles Graphics, 1994.

_____ Notes *of a Crucian Son.* St. Croix: Antilles Graphics, 1989.

_____ *Under De Taman Tree.* St. Croix: Antilles Graphics, 1996.

Simmonds, Bodil Mason. Christiansted, St. Croix. Interview, 4 May, 2021.

St. Croix Christmas Festival Booklets, St. Croix. 1953 – 1960.

Thomas, Lydia Nico. Christiansted, St. Croix. Interview, 23 February, 2022.

Thurland, Karen C. "Kill Ting Pappy." *Crucian Xmas Fiesta 82-83: Thirty Years of Cultural Heritage – Bright as Ever.* 1982.

Thurland, Karen C. *The Neighborhoods of Christiansted, St. Croix: 1910 -1960.* Bloomington, IN: Author House, 2009.

_____ *The Sugar Industry on St. Croix.* Bloomington, IN: Author House, 2014.

_____ *Tradesmen of St. Croix.* Bloomington, IN: Author House, 2018.

Thraen, Yvonne Dr. St. Thomas, Virgin Islands. Interview, 9 May, 2021.

Valls, Lito. *What a Pistarckle! A Dictionary of Virgin Islands English Creole.* St. John, USVI: Lito Valls, 1990.

Virgin Islands Council on the Arts. *Arts in the U.S. Virgin Islands.* No date.

Williams, Asta. Frederiksted, St. Croix. Interview, 20 April, 2021.

# ABOUT THE AUTHOR

Karen C. Thurland, Ph.D., of Christiansted, St. Croix, U.S. Virgin Islands, is an educator, historian and author. She is the author of *The Thurland Family and the Furniture Making Tradition, Peter G. Thurland: Master Cabinetmaker and Bandleader, The 872nd and 873rd Port Companies: My Father's Story, The Neighborhoods of Christiansted: 1910-1970, The Sugar Industry on St. Croix, and Tradesmen of St. Croix: U.S. Virgin Islands.* She is the daughter of Will and Modesta Larsen Thurland of St. Croix. Karen is a 1998 recipient of the Governor's Award for Excellence in the Arts in the United States Virgin Islands.

Printed in the United States
by Baker & Taylor Publisher Services